him, Him, and hymn

him, Him, and hymn

A Women's Guide to Pain, Blame, and Recovery

Book 1: The Trilogy Series

KRISTINA KAY

PALMETTO PUBLISHING

Charleston, SC
www.PalmettoPublishing.com

him, Him, and hymn

Copyright © 2023 by KristinaKay3 LLC

First Edition

Paperback ISBN: 979-8-8229-1290-8

Unless otherwise indicated, all Scripture quotations are taken from the *The Holy Bible*, NEW INTERNATIONAL VERSION®, NIV® Copyright ©1973, 1978, 1984, 2011, 2019 by Biblica, Inc.® Used by permission. All rights reserved worldwide.

Scripture quotations marked (NLT) are taken from the *Holy Bible*, New Living Translation, copyright ©1996, 2004, 2015 by Tyndale House Foundation. Used by permission of Tyndale House Publishers, Carol Stream, Illinois 60188. All rights reserved.

"Rescue" written by Jason Ingram, Lauren Daigle, and Paul Mabury Copyright ©2018 CentricSongs (SESAC) See You At The Pub (SESAC) (adm. at CapitolCMGPublishing.com) All rights reserved. Used by permission.

"You Say" written by Jason Ingram, Lauren Daigle, Bebo Norman, Michael Morgan Donehey, and Paul Mabury Copyright ©2018 CentricSongs (SESAC) See You at the Pub (SESAC) Appstreet Music (ASCAP)(adm. at CapitolCMGPublishing.com) All rights reserved. Used by permission.

"Trust in You" written by Lauren Daigle, Michael Farren, and Paul Mabury Copyright ©2014 CentricSongs (SESAC) See You At The Pub (SESAC) (adm. at CapitolCMGPublishing.com) All rights reserved. Used by permission.

"Rescue written" by Jason Ingram* / Paul Mabury* / Lauren Daigle ©2018 So Essential Tunes (SESAC) / Fellow Ships Music (SESAC) / ICM Crescendo Royalty Publishing (SESAC) (admin at EssentialMusicPublishing.com). All rights reserved. Used by permission.

"Trust in You" written by Paul Mabury* / Lauren Daigle / Michael Farren ©2015 Oceans Away Music (SESAC) / So Essential Tunes (SESAC) (admin at EssentialMusicPublishing.com). All rights reserved. Used by permission.

"You Say" written by Paul Mabury* / Jason Ingram* / Lauren Daigle / Michael Donehey* / Bebo Norman ©2015 Oceans Away Music (SESAC) / So Essential Tunes (SESAC) (admin at EssentialMusicPublishing.com). All rights reserved. Used by permission.

* Denotes a controlled songwriter.

Dedication

There are so many people in my life that have supported me during the creation of this book, and I am so grateful to you all. However, I have to dedicate this one to my boys, the "hims" that make my life worth living. I literally may not have survived without you guys by my side. Thank you both so much for your love and support but also for the days you made me laugh and held me when I cried. Continue to keep God first in your lives and in your relationships. I love you to the moon and back, and I will always love you more!

Table of Contents

Why This Book?

When I was a little girl, I loved to write. I wrote poems, songs (usually with my big brother), letters, and stories. We moved around a ton growing up, and somewhere down the line, my compilation of childhood writings got lost. Oh, what I would do to have those now! I was the girl who wrote letters to her friends and boyfriends to say I love you or to say I was sorry. You remember the days when people used paper and pencils to communicate? To this day there is nothing better than holding an actual paper letter, note, or book. When I met the man that would later become my husband, I started a journal to tell our story. I described the adventures of building a relationship, the good and the ugly, as well as how my heart grew as I fell truly in love for the first time. I wrote the journal as a dedication to the man I eventually married, who I once called my Knight in Shining Armor. This journal continued till our one-year anniversary when I excitedly switched over to writing a journal about the experience of pregnancy and childbirth. I completed that journey on my first son's first birthday. The excitement and fear of becoming a mother for the first time drove my entries. The dedication that time was to my son. He is now a young adult and not ready to appreciate it yet, but I pray someday he and hopefully his future wife will. When my son was two years old, I found out I was expecting our second. A new writing adventure began. Would I be able to love this child as much? Would the pregnancy be the same? Again, I wrapped up the story at my second son's first birthday. And yes, of course I love my peanut as much as his big brother, but in a different, unique to us way. Each experience was the same and different. Each child holds a special place in my heart, and the youngest too will someday be ready to read about the joys and fears I felt becoming his mother.

I allowed my busy working-mom-and-wife life take me away from my passion, which we all probably do. I still wrote letters and cards to my husband to say I love you or I am sorry. It has always been how I open up best. I eventually found a new outlet via social media posts. Facebook became my canvas. I loved sharing our family's adventures with friends and family. I was always honest about the difficult times as well. Why? It was research, networking, and a call for help. Sharing about our hardships led people to open up about theirs, which often made me feel not so alone. When my oldest was diagnosed at age six with ADD, epilepsy, and Chiari malformation, it shocked me the people I knew who had been there too. The support was amazing! Same situation when my youngest was found to have fifteen allergies, one being anaphylactic, and severe asthma. People shared their stories, advice, doctors' names, alternative foods, and medicines, and most importantly, people sent prayers. Oftentimes I hear people say that others share too much on social media. "Why would they put something so personal out there?" and "They are just looking for attention!" This may be true, but maybe it is their call for help or just cheap therapy. I never judge because I understand. So, if you are a social media junky like me, think about that before you unfriend or speak ill of another's post.

Instead, just scroll on by or even better yet consider reaching out or saying a prayer for them.

Most recently I picked up the pen and a journal again when my husband of twenty years asked for a divorce because *he* no longer loved me. Ouch is right! We will get into that more later (bet you can't wait). This was a painful reintroduction to writing. I poured my heart out onto the pages while trying my best to be as strong as I could in front of my boys and my family (usually failing). It was during this that God took over. Do not get me wrong, *He* has always been there. *He* has always spoken to me, but I have not always listened (sound familiar?). As I prayed, *He* told me to write. As I wrote, *He* told me to share. As I shared, *He* told me to publish. Say what? Like write a book? For the whole world to see? *He* demanded, "YES!" Then the rationalizing and excuses began. Now is not the time. I am not ready. I have no experience. Who am I to publish a book? As I procrastinated and hid behind the excuses, *He* continued to get in my face, as God will do when you do not listen. So here I am, writing my first book. *He* has given me answers to some of my questions. I am me. I have been through many things, and I am willing and able to share about them in order to help others (and also get a little therapy for myself in the process). No, I am not an expert in anything. No, I am not well rehearsed in the art of professional writing or research. And no, I am not as wise or as well-versed biblically as I would like to be, but God has shown me that these are the reasons why I need to write to you. *He* said that I would connect easier with you and you with me because we are all simply the same: learners, sinners, and searchers.

Did you know that Noah was not a carpenter? However, God called *him* to build a magnificent ark in Genesis. Let us pray this book doesn't take me several decades to complete, though! Also, sweet little David was not a fighter like *his* big brothers, *he* was just a shepherd boy. However, in 1 Samuel *he* defeats Goliath with no fear because *he* had faith in God. In 1 Samuel 17:45–46, David says to the freakishly big, bad, scary Philistine warrior *he* is about to kill, "You come against me with sword and spear and javelin, but I come against you in the name of the LORD Almighty, the God of the armies of Israel, whom you have defied. This day the LORD will deliver you into my hands, and I will strike you down and cut off your head." That is gutsy! Can't you just hear Goliath laughing at David? Well, David did exactly as *he* predicted. So, I will use my computer, pen, and paper to fight off the evil in my world with God's support and guidance. Lastly, I want to bring attention to the fisherman and businessman, Peter, who wrote two books of the Bible, as well as discipled John Mark before *he* wrote the book of Mark. Peter was not a writer by profession just like many others who were called to author a book of the Bible. I could go on and on about the people in the Bible who were called to do things by God that were not in their prospective wheelhouses, but guess what? They did it and were successful because they had faith. By faith I, a schoolteacher and mother, answer God's call to write this book and write it now. So instead of being on the other end of the devastating divorce process where I can give you a happy ending about how it was the right thing for me and things are amazing on the other side, I am writing in the thick of it, sharing the process with you. Let's be real, even though it is most likely true, it is hard to hear all the good that will supposedly come at the end of a storm, even harder to believe. Sometimes we just need to feel the pain and wallow in it a bit. However, I hope by the end of this book you, and I, find comfort and strength in God's words. Know that though I do not feel I am worthy of giving you advice or answers, I know that God is. I am an instrument in *His* work. My prayer is that *He* uses me to help you and you to help me.

Pray with me now:

> Heavenly Father, I ask that *You* open my heart to *Your* words. That the experiences of others can help me understand and have no fear. That I will see how *You* work and understand that *You* have a plan for me and my future. Help me to use *Your* word as guidance in my decisions and to have the utmost faith in *You*. Use this book to give me peace, help me not feel alone, and to grow closer to *You*, Lord. In *Your* glorious name I pray. Amen.

Trilogy Introduction

I am not even sure when *He* first spoke to me about writing a book. Actually, it probably was years and years ago. I have always wanted to but never knew how or what it would be about. God started planning this book with me while I sat in church (sorry, Pastor Andy). I found I had become extremely attention deficit during services. God would not shut up in my ear. "OK, OK, I give in!" I began talking about the ideas that *He* was flooding into my brain with my wonderful, supportive, Godly mother. This was step one. Then Mom began to question me on a regular basis, a little motherly push and nudge in the right direction that, as you know of mothers, was nothing close to subtle. The first thing God gave me was the title *him, Him, and hymn* because we often struggle to know when things are happening because of the common man, *him*, or when it is God's will, *Him*. Also, because the one part of the church service I was always able to focus on was the music. I had been raised in a musical family. I unfortunately did not inherit one lick of the talent; God poured all that into my brother. However, the appreciation for it is deeply instilled in my bones. This is the "why" for the last *hymn*. As the months passed, I sat in the rows at church, and God fed me ideas (sorry, Pastor Gavin). The series would be called *The*

Trilogy Series, always based on three main components and the last always being music. Excuse me, now it's a series? Yep, that is what *He* wants.

I would love to say I am an avid reader, but sadly I am not. I want to be, though. I do, however, read many, many children's books (did I mention I am an elementary school teacher?). I have read some big people books too; some I am not so proud of, but hey, maybe that was part of my learning process. During this call to write, the Lord has put many religious writers in my path. I have read, listened to blogs, watched videos, as well as done Bible studies that have given me guidance. Mind you this is all new to me. I went years and years without reading or writing. I am ashamed to say this, but it is important for you to know because I am probably a lot like you. I really had to fight to make reading and my studying a priority. Grocery shopping, the gym, work, the kids, the husband, the pets, TV, and sadly the phone all took precedence over what God wanted me to be doing. But there is never a better time to start fitting in some you-and-God time than now. I cannot get up early! I hate mornings! So, for me, God time was on weekend days or weeknights, but not too late because I am getting older and dark means sleep. But I digress, back to the setup of the book and hopefully, if you all like this one, the books yet to come.

Three parts (hence trilogy). I purposely want to make this thing short. Few of us have time, patience, or the attention for long chapters or books. I discovered that even when reading things I enjoy, I look ahead to when the chapter is over, and I get to go to sleep. If it is too lengthy, I tend to start skimming or skipping to finish. This work will be compiled of shorter parts that are manageable and hopefully keep your attention. I definitely do not want you skimming my pages to find the end! The three main parts will be broken into three mini sections, each with a prayer at the end. I will ask you questions to ponder but nothing you have to write down. I will, however, place journal pages at the end of each section for you to write down your thoughts and feelings if you choose. As I have stated, I am a journaler. I believe journaling is good therapy. So, the lines will be there if you want to give it a go or grab a journal you have written in, are writing in, or go buy a pretty new one to jot down your thoughts while reading. The final section will contain why the music I have chosen helped me and about the words of the songs. Hopefully, you will download and listen to them (if you haven't already) and find your own connections to each song. My last promise to you is that if I refer to a verse of the Bible, I will give it to you. Ain't nobody got time to look it up, and if you are like me, you probably wouldn't anyway.

And there you have it, a book like no other, hopefully, God willing, to be a series like no other. Thank you so much for taking this journey with me. I pray you enjoy reading it as much as I hope to enjoy writing it.

Now let our adventure begin!

him

PART ONE:

him

Part One will contain three sections on the "hims" in our lives. These will be about *him*, *her*, and *them*. I am referring to the people in our lives that may have hurt us or done us wrong. The generic *him* was used on purpose because *them, Him, and hymn* would not have been nearly as catchy of a title. When we first get wronged, we immediately focus on what the other person did. We begin to list the reasons they are so bad. Don't get me wrong, often what they are doing is bad, but this isn't very healthy for us to dwell on. No worries, I am going to let you soak in the anger a bit. I think it is cathartic, part of the healing process. However, I hope by the end of the book to bring us out of it and show how we need to also look within ourselves for our part, if any, and how we can better surround ourselves with the *hims, hers,* and *thems* God put in our lives. "In your anger do not sin. Do not let the sun go down while you are still angry and do not give the devil a foot-hold" (Ephesians 4:26–27).

Pray with me now for God to speak to us during this touchy and at times uncomfortable part of the book.

Wondrous Father, please use real-life stories to help me relate to the Biblical stories *You* selectively chose to be worthy enough to have written and shared for thousands of years. God open my heart to my part in my hurt, show me the way to healing. Also, Lord help me to forgive the *hims*, *hers*, and *thems* that have wounded me as *You* have forgiven me for the times I have wounded *You*. Guide me in letting go of anger and not allowing it to cause me to sin. In *Your* magnificent name I pray. Amen.

PART 1-1:

The D Word

I struggled with writing a book about divorce. I didn't want to be yet another one of "those books." However, some of "those books" have helped me not feel alone. Not to mention, God said to me, "YOU WILL SHARE YOUR STORY," in his booming voice over and over again. Wasn't going to say no to *Him*. My next dilemma was not wanting to hurt my children or even my STBX (soon-to-be ex) in the process. Maybe that was why it was important to write now. I am not in the hating stage of divorce, which is normal if you are because there are many stages to this crazy drama. Did you know that the stages of grief are fluid? Nobody's process is exactly the same, and that is OK. I was in the anger stage for like a second and will most definitely go back to it again (probably multiple times before finishing this book), but for now I still love *him* and assume I always will in some way. So, this part will be about my divorce, but don't worry, I won't dwell on it the entire book. Also, I am well aware there are two sides to every story, so keep in mind, this is mine.

Let me start by saying I do not regret a second of the last twenty-three years I spent with my husband—*he* was my best friend, my confidant, my everything! We traveled, experienced many firsts together, we were blessed with two amazing (if I do say so myself) sons, and we bought three beautiful homes. We even went to church together; my STBX is a Christian too. But life gets hairy. We both have always been hardheaded, always wanting to be right. Since the D word started, someone said to me, "Is it better to be right or happy?" Wish I would have had that little lesson sooner. My husband and I are alike in many ways. Maybe the "opposites attract" thing should say "opposites last." Things were not always perfect in our marriage (not a shocking statement probably, it is marriage after all). We began really pulling away from each other just six short months before our twentieth anniversary. A new house, a graduating oldest son, and running a successful business was all weighing on our marriage. Not to mention *him* turning fifty was right around the corner. It was definitely obvious to us both we were in turmoil. The conversation of divorce did happen, but I was going to fight for us. This is totally in my personality, I am a fighter, which is both a good and bad characteristic. I bought us Christian marriage books to read and begged *him* to join a small group at church so *he* could see we are not abnormal in our roller coaster of emotions for each other (though *he* was not on board for either of those things). *he* did go away with me for a weekend, threw me a great forty-third birthday party, and agreed to counseling, though short-lived. Twenty-eight days before our twentieth anniversary, *he* woke me up one morning and shook my world by saying, "I don't love you anymore." Those words cut deeper than any sword could! I honestly didn't see it coming. I foolishly thought things were improving. And here is how fast my life flipped upside down: a day later I told my parents, two days later we told our sons, one week later *he* moved out. *he* is a "flighter" (yep, that is surely a word, don't question me, teacher, remember?). Let me be clear; I asked *him* to leave the house because *he* said there was no hope and would not keep working toward a resolution. The "flighter" thing isn't specifically related to the leaving of the home but leaving our family and our marriage. I seriously don't get the idea of "I am breaking your heart and ruining our future but let's be room-mates." Maybe that works for others, but I couldn't do that to myself or my kids. I wasn't looking to lose a husband and gain a roommate all in one day. That just felt awkward. Plus, if I was getting a roomie, it was going to be someone who loved to clean and do laundry (can I get an amen, ladies?)! This brings me to the now, drowning in the painful holiday season and the discovery stage (paperwork overkill) of the D word.

At first, I was ashamed to admit that I begged *him* to stay. I crawled onto *his* lap and pleaded with *him* to love me again; I would have done anything. Now I see that I hold no shame. I went down fighting. I even sent him a letter, the card I wrote *him* on our wedding day (see me and writing), and a peace lily on our twentieth anniversary to his new apartment. In response, a day later, I got a "thanks" text (imagine my face when all I received back was that). I tried everything in my power, and I am proud that someday my boys will look back on that and see I fought for my marriage and our family. So, what else was there to do now than to play the blame game? *he* didn't try! *he* gave up! *he* hadn't loved me in a while. *he* left his family. And then I started reaching for straws. I know you know what that is like. There must be another woman! Maybe *he* lost a bunch of money gambling and did not want to tell me. Maybe *he* is an alcoholic. I ached for one of these horrid things to be true about the man I loved only because I thought it would make it easier on me. I wanted answers! Let me be clear, though, for those of you who know you were cheated on, were or are being abused, or lied to; I don't claim for a sec-ond that is easy on you. I am sure it was or still is miserable and unfair. I thank God every day that though this is painful, I know it could be worse, and I have to realize and accept that I may never understand the why. I have a big heart but have always led with my head; I inherited that from my daddy. I analyze, postulate, and need solutions to problems. Having no clear-cut answer beyond "*he* doesn't love me" was killing me! So no, we may not always get the answers we are searching for, but God says in 1 Thessalonians 5:18, "give thanks in all circumstances; for this is God's will for you in Christ Jesus." Say what? This is God's will? How many of you cried out "WHY GOD?" a thousand times during a grieving process? Well, we will get to *His* role in all this in Part 2. For now, what I want you to know is it was *his* decision to leave me, not *His*. God gives man free will. *He* allows us to make our own choices, good and bad. Know the difference between what *he* did and what *He* did in your life. *He* did not cause the divorce, but *He* may have allowed it. Place blame where blame belongs, but don't spend too much time conjuring up make-believe reasons as to why. It will drive you mad! Some things we are not to know or understand. Recognize when it is time to let it go and move forward with your new life. I am very fond of social media memes and inspirational quotes. One that really got to me on this subject was that losing someone alive is oftentimes harder than if they had died. Harsh, right? But also, kind of true. This is called ambiguous grief. Think about it, if *he* did not choose to leave me, wouldn't it be easier to grieve him? Now I run around town afraid of answering the phone or seeing *him* in public and feeling rejected and embarrassed. Ugh, DIVORCE stinks! However, know what the Lord said to Joshua when *he* was going into the fight of his life against five kings and their armies: "Do not be afraid of them..." (Joshua 10:8). Proverbs 29:25 reminds us that "fear of man will prove to be a snare, but whoever trusts in the Lord is kept safe." If you are not sure who you can trust, know you can trust in the Lord,

His word, and *His* plan for you. There is one last verse I want to bring to your attention on the subject of fear, which I get is so real and hard to get under control. It is found in the hymnbook of Psalms in verses 118:5-9:

> In my anguish I cried to the Lord, and the Lord answered by setting me free. The Lord is with me, I will not be afraid. What can man do to me? The Lord is with me; He is my helper. I will look in triumph on my enemies.

Pretty self-explanatory, right? So, no more fearing your ex or current significant other! *he* is just a man. Let God handle *him*, you worry about you. Face *him* with your head held high. Look at *him* with strength in your eyes and the Lord in your heart. Do not yell, blame, or call *him* names. Speak to *him* with words that honor God and you. Isn't that what Jesus would do? I know this takes practice, and if you are like me, you will have to ask God for a great deal of forgiveness and strength until you finally get it under control. Know that is okay. God understands our individual process and suffering and will grant you both, like *He* did for me.

Let's talk more about *his* role in a marriage from a biblical standpoint. There are many verses about a husband's role in marriage in Ephesians. The apostle Paul wrote the book of Ephesians as a letter to the church and to the people of Ephesus. *he* wanted them to know how to live a life that honored the Lord. This is a powerful excerpt from Paul's letter:

> Husbands, love your wives, just as Christ loved the church and gave himself up for her to make her holy, cleansing her by the washing with water through the word, and to present her to himself as a radiant church, without stain or wrinkle

or any other blemish, but holy and blameless. In this same way husbands are to love their wives as their own bodies. He who loves his wife, loves himself. For this reason, a man will leave his father and mother and be united to his wife, and the two will become one flesh. (Ephesians 5:25–28, 31)

Paul also wrote a similar letter to the Corinthian people. These verses are used all the time in wedding ceremonies, cards, and even home décor. So obviously they are pretty powerful. The most well-known of these is 1 Corinthians 13:4–8:

Love is patient, love is kind, it does not envy, it does not boast, it is not proud. It is not rude, it is not self-seeking, it is not easily angered, it keeps no records of wrongs. Love does not delight in evil but rejoices with the truth. It always protects, always trusts, always hopes, always preserves. Love never fails.

Those words are especially meaningful to me because they were read during my parents' wedding. They have been married for fifty years. My maternal and paternal grandparents were married till death did they part; both reached over fifty years! We do not see that monumental golden anniversary as much nowadays. My parents and grandparents have all told me about some pretty hairy times in their marriages (there may have even been a knife-throwing story and an ugly song written about leaving). There were times they questioned their own feelings and each other's, but they never gave up. They were and still are my role models for marriage, and I really felt like I was on the same track as them. Guess not (the writer declares with a sad face). Talk about confusion. I thought love never failed. If the love spoken about in Corinthians is the true definition of real love, then only it never fails. It is not easy getting all those things right, but with patience, forgiveness, and understanding for one another, it can happen. We can have that special, once-in-a-lifetime kind of relationship like my parents and grandparents.

Paul wrote yet another letter to the Church of Colossae, and in Colossians 3:19 he wrote, "Husbands love your wives, and do not be harsh with them." I know some of you are feeling justified right now, probably nodding your head and yelling, "Preach, Paul!" Oftentimes *he* may use *his* authority, size, or strength as a weapon against you. Yes, that is awfully harsh and against God's will. The purpose of these letters was to teach the people of the church the way to have a relationship that honors Christ. You will see Paul talks about what us gals have to do as well in the next section. I know you can't wait for that (insert eye roll).

Lastly, on Godly husbands' duties, I want to discuss 1 Peter 3:7: "Husbands, in the same way be considerate as you live with your wives and treat them with respect as the weaker partner...." I bet some of you are all up in arms over that one. Listen, if ever there were a woman-power-kinda gal, it is me. But let me explain. Women and men were created differently, on purpose, starting all the way back with Eve who was created from Adam's rib. They have different roles, strengths, and weaknesses that were made to complement each other. In general, women are not as strong physically by design. Furthermore, let me be the first to admit I might, sometimes, sort of be an emotional bomb ready to go off at any minute. This is not meant as an insult by Peter or God, but as a way of saying be her protector. I for one loved feeling that protection from my husband. I felt safe in *his* arms. I knew *he* would never let anyone harm me. Who knew in the end *he* would be the one that did?

9

Did you know divorce existed in the Bible? Researching it was one of the first things I did. Not that research would bring *him* back. I longed for that in my heart but knew in my head *he* was not returning to me. So why the research? Well, I am glad you asked. I was afraid of my future. What will become of me now? How will this work in the eyes of God and the church? So, what does the Bible say? Malachi questions (in more of a statement kind of way), "Didn't the Lord make you one with your wife? In body and spirit you are his" (Malachi 2:15, NLT). Then God states, "For I hate divorce!" "To divorce your wife is to over-whelm her with cruelty" (Malachi 2:16, NLT). Some translations state it as not God saying, "I hate," but a warning if man hates and divorces his wife, *he* is doing a violent act to the one *he* should protect. Oh yeah, I like that. "Man," you are supposed to protect us! However, there are times in the Bible that Moses allowed divorces, not that God did not still feel saddened by it. Remember that just because it happened in the Bible does not mean God approved of it. If a woman was adulterous for exam-ple, Moses, who delivered the word from God, allowed man to serve *his* wife a certificate of divorce. These stories are found numerous times in the Bible, and the fact that the certificate had to be served is always of importance. These certificates are mentioned again in Matthew 5:31, Mark 19:8-9, Isaiah 50:1, and Jeremiah 3:8. In the book of Matthew, we are reminded by Jesus Christ that this was not the original intention of God. Jesus says in Matthew 19:8, "... 'Moses permitted you to divorce your wives because your hearts were hard. But it was not this way from the beginning.'" See, woman was created to be with man because man needed a partner in life. This was the de-sign, in life and for life. The disciples then question if it wouldn't be easier then to just never marry. Jesus explains that mar-riage may not be for everyone and that those who cannot abide by the laws of being married forever, under God, should then be "eunuchs." Bet you have never heard that word. Well, let me enlighten you. A eunuch is a male who has been castrated or neutered (I know where your mind just went, and no, ladies, this is not an option). This was especially seen in the days when men were employed to guard a women's bedroom. Think of the old movies you watch about kings and queens and princesses and knights. Jesus explains that some men are born that way (meaning born unable to produce offspring) or choose to live that way for the purpose of honoring and reaping the rewards of the Kingdom of Heaven. But back to that piece of paper. What if there was no adultery on the women's part? What if *he* did not want to serve divorce papers? What if *he* was adulterous or cruel or if *he* did not fulfill his husbandly duties? What if *he* is not a Godly man? What if (like in my case) *he* stopped loving you? What can we as women do?

Do you have any thoughts on these questions? Did I conjure up any other questions or ideas about your own marriage, current or past relationships? Feel free to write them on the journaling pages following this section. Also, maybe you just want to rant, to tell your story, or scribble loudly. Go ahead. Get it out! These are your pages to use as you see fit. I promise that writing it down helps you to heal, at least it has me.

Pray with me now:

> Lord my Father, I may not always have answers
> but help me to have faith in *You*. Help me to use
> my story to help others and to grow myself. Help
> me to use *Your* words found in the stories of the
> Bible to try to understand man, marriage, and
> divorce. Teach me when to let go of the what-
> ifs and trust in *Your* plan. Allow me to grieve
> safely and recognize when it is time to move on.
> Help me to discern what is *his* doing and what is
> *Yours*. In *Your* powerful name. Amen.

BE A JOURNALER!

BE A JOURNALER!

PART 1-2:

Could It Be Me

After *he* had left, I was struggling to move on. As I see it, we have three roads to choose from when hurt: *him* (depression, not getting over him, and dwelling in the misery), *them* (partying with friends or maybe not even friends to try to forget the pain), and *Him* (turning to the word of God to find peace and happiness again). I drove down all the roads for a hot minute but have been happily cruising down *His* road for a while now, and the view is much nicer. I pray if you are traveling down one of the other two, you will now turn back. They are not the way to happiness and fulfillment! At first, I sat around waiting for the D word papers to be served, but *he* stated *he* was too busy, and the papers didn't really mean anything to *him*. I have heard from lawyers, counselors, and other divorcées that this is common from men during a divorce. What do we as Christian women do then? My STBX husband has said to me and others many times that *he* knew I would never be the one to divorce because of my beliefs. *he* was correct; I did not and still do not believe in divorce as the easy way out of a marriage. Marriage takes work; it is messy. Biblically the Old Testament states some of the laws of marriage and basic needs each is to provide to the other. For example, the wife is to provide meals and clothing (eeks, right off the bat

I falter; cooking was never my forte, but I can shop for clothes like nobody's business). Husbands are to provide protection and food. Both husband and wife are to LOVE each other. What if those needs are not met? I searched the Bible, talked to my spiritual mentors, and reached out to the church for answers.

First and foremost, I needed to see my part in all this. The first road I took was extremely unhealthy. I share it in hopes of keeping you from spiraling down the same path or at the least make you see you are not alone if you did. I blamed me. Before I even started the blame game on *him*. "I must have been awful to live with! I am very OCD. I did not cook for him enough. I didn't give him what he needed emotionally and physically." This sent me into a deep depression. My wifely duties and mothering skills were put on trial, and I was judging myself. I was in extreme pain. Bet you can relate to that. I cried and contemplated suicide, not once but twice. What you need to understand about suicide is though it is said to be a selfish act, the person in that moment has lost sense of reality and truly feels it is selfless, what is best for everyone, and the only way to end their suffering. I did not fully act on it but got very close once. I had even written the suicide notes to my kids, parents, and STBX in my head. I knew the how (different both times) and got all the way to the moment of, but then God happened. Both times God was my lifeline and made me phone a friend—well, once a cousin, once a friend. That took mad humility and vulnerability to do. It wasn't attention seeking. I really didn't want to make the call. Honestly, God made me do it. There I was, a middle-class, well-educated schoolteacher, mother, and wife hitting rock bottom. Goes to show depression does not discriminate. I got help ASAP! Found myself in the doctor's office the next day getting prescriptions for depression and anxiety followed by counseling appointments that I have stuck with regularly to this day. I needed help and that was OK. Actually, the strongest thing I have done to this point was getting help. If you need help, please for the love of all that is woman, get it! You are worth living; you are not to shoulder the blame alone. "Cast all your anxiety on him because he cares for you" (1 Peter 5:7). You are beautiful, and you matter to God, to me, and to others!

Next, and once I was stronger, was to find my part in all this in a healthier way. Did I put God first in my marriage? Nope! Did I put my husband second? Nope! But we both were guilty of this. Children especially tend to creep up that ladder and beat each other out. If you are still working on your marriage while reading this or for future relationships, do not forget to date your significant other, always. Not just in a group or family outings but just the two of you. It is so important to your relationship and growth. At the healthiest and happiest time of our marriage, we regularly went to dinner and movies and even rotated vacations with the kids and just the two of us. Also, you should pray together. I cannot emphasize enough how important that is, even if it seems uncomfortable to do. It was for me. I always had to start it, and it seemed awkward, so I just stopped asking. Don't stop asking *him* to pray with you! Sometimes jobs, friends, or unhealthy things also find their way ahead in the pecking order. One thing I was shocked to realize was that I was worshipping golden idols and comparing my husband to them. No way, right? I bet that seems one of the things you can say without question you are not doing or have not done. If you watch romance movies, TV shows, or even read books that portray the male figure as "all that" and find yourself wishing your husband was more like *them*, you too are guilty. Hold on to your hats, ladies, it is now time to read what our friend Paul says in his letters about a woman's role in the marriage.

In Ephesians Paul writes, "...the wife must respect her husband"(5:33). This brings me to the "love, honor, and obey" part of my wedding vows. I remember being so "Women Power" that I said the "and obey" part a bit sarcastically at my wedding, and people laughed. Worst of all it is on video! However, what I have learned is that when a Godly husband abides by the laws of marriage and sacrifices for *his* wife the way Jesus sacrificed for the church, a Godly woman will want to obey and respect *him.* It will just come naturally. So, if man is "...temperate, worthy of respect, self-controlled, and sound in faith, in love and endurance" (Titus 2:2), then women will want to "love their husbands and children, to be self-controlled and pure, to be busy at home, to be kind, and subject to their husbands..." (Titus 2:4). Oh, and FYI, Paul also wrote Titus as a letter to Titus, his brother in Christ, a Christian missionary, and leader. The statements above were describing what should be taught to the men and women in the church so that they may teach it to future generations of men and women. Makes me think what I want my kids to learn about marriage and divorce. Am I teaching them the right things? I pray for that all the time. But again, I digress. Maybe that is a topic for a future book.

So, let's get to the nitty-gritty. Was I being a good wife? I thought so but maybe not good enough; that is harsh but true. I do believe it was in response to not feeling like I was getting what I needed, but *he* probably felt the same way. So then when, where, and how does it start? In my mind, and biblically too by the way, it is with the man of the house. The husband is to be the leader of the home and marriage, you know, like the Bible says. But in the case when the man is not Godly or at least not as Godly as the woman, is it her job to step it up? Yep, it sure is! "For a believing husband is made holy because of his wife..." (1 Corinthians 7:14 ESV); "...wives, be subject to your own husbands, so that even if some do not obey the word, they may be won without a word by the conduct of their wives" (1 Peter 3:1). That basically means keep your mouth shut and lead a Christian life. God will take *him* from there. The problem is that oftentimes women are pulled into the nonpracticing or nonbeliever's lifestyle instead. This makes God sad but the devil very happy. The devil's strength in our relationships is often ignored. Satan wants us to lead each other away from God and for love to fail. This has literally been the case since the beginning of time. Look at what the serpent did to Adam and Eve in Genesis. Satan in the form of a slithering snake pitted them against each other as they had to explain their disobedience (the first sins noted in the Bible) to God. Don't let Satan in! Stay strong in your faith, ladies. Get up and go to church even if alone. Lead the family in prayer. Say no to going out, partying, watching something inappropriate, or being around people who you feel are not healthy for you and your relationship. Say no!

As I mentioned earlier, the paperwork was not happening fast enough for me. It did not seem to take priority for *him*. What if the man does not give that mentioned certificate of divorce? What if *he* does not hold up *his* duties or love *his* wife? Well, the good news is women are allowed to take action. I studied and searched what steps I could take. My mentors in Christ (mostly consisting of my family or friend) said *he* left the marriage already; the rest was just semantics. But how did I know *they* weren't just concerned for me and speaking what *they* thought I should do, not what God wanted me to do? Then a counselor from my church said that I was not going to hear the words "Go ahead and file" from anyone at the church. However, she counseled me on God knowing my heart, the past, and the future. She said I needed to only care about what *He* guides me to do and how I feel in the end will be my answer. I prayed multiple times a day for guidance and peace about whatever decision I was to make. At the beginning of this all, *He* kept showing me, "Be still..." (Psalm 46:10). Being still is not my thing! I struggle with patience: red lights, traffic, lines, and taking turns—I hate it all! But my friends were giving me cards, pictures, and even a necklace with those powerful words inscribed on them. I waited till God showed me what to do. Let me tell you *He* was smacking me over the head with it the entire time, but once again, I was not listening. I should have focused on the rest of the Psalms verse, "...and know that I am God." No matter what I did, *He* would forgive me if I asked. *He* knew my future; *He* knew what I was going to do all along. The "be still..." part of that verse does not translate into literally don't move or lie on the couch and wait (or in my case cry and eat). It means to not worry, to pray, and then to trust in *Him*. So, I did. *He* showed me a sign that I could not ignore (because *He* knew I needed a big, neon, flashing one to get my attention), and I filed for divorce three months after *he* left. When I left the lawyer's office that day, I had a peace about me I had not felt in a very long time. And only after the fact did God show me Exodus 21:10-11 where it states that the Law of Moses commands a divorce if a husband fails to provide for his wife "food, clothing, and marital rights," which includes LOVE. Also, I uncovered when the apostle Paul allowed for divorce for abandonment in 1 Corinthians 7:14-15. There are actually multiple times in the Bible where divorce is allowed. And to make me feel a little better about being titled the horrific term, "a divorcée," God himself is one. In Jeremiah 3:8 the Lord states, "I gave faithless Israel her certificate of divorce and sent her away because of all her adulteries."

As we wrap up our part in marriage and divorce, be honest with yourself. What could you have done better? What do you take responsibility for? What do you think made you act this way? How can you grow from this now? Did *he* fulfill *his* martial duties, did you? Remember, these journal pages are just for your eyes. *he* will never know (and *He* already does) what you admit to (unless you are like me, in which case you put it out there for the entire world to read).

Please pray with me.

> Heavenly Counselor, I thank *You* for *Your* words. Thank *You* for using Paul's letters to speak to me about my part in a marriage and possibly my part in the divorce. Help me to admit my wrongdoings, to grow from my mistakes, and to forgive myself. Please, Lord, forgive me for my sins in the marriage and in the divorce. Aid me in following *Your* will from this point forward and to act more like the Godly woman Paul has described in his letters. In *Your* forgiving name I pray. Amen.

BE A JOURNALER!

BE A JOURNALER!

_____

_____

_____

_____

_____

_____

_____

_____

_____

_____

_____

_____

_____

_____

_____

_____

_____

_____

_____

_____

_____

_____

_____

_____

PART 1-3:

Friends in Low and High Places

As promised, I will not just talk about you and your relationship with your spouse or significant other. What about the friends in your life that you feel have done you wrong, the *hers* and the *thems*? Well, I have some doozies (don't we all?). I was warned at the beginning of this whole mess, from those who have been through it, that people would come out of the woodwork to "support me" but really just wanted the gossip and would later disappear. Also, some would choose *his* side and would no longer be my friends. Umm, not my friends! Surely everyone will see I am the victim here. I mean come on, there is no choice to make. The sad, caring, kind wife who did not want it or the big, bad husband who did. Well, two sides to every story, remember?

There have been "friends" in my past that have told lies about us and tried to get in between our marriage. We survived it, though. There have been those that have just faded away, as friends sometimes do. All those hurt me. They hurt because I love my friends deeply. I have been raised to love unconditionally. I mean, isn't it the easiest of *His* commands,

"Love one another as I have loved you"(John 15:12)? Apparently, it is not that easy for some. Relationships of all kinds take work and at all ages. People grow apart for many reasons. Most of them would be welcomed back into my circle (which has gotten much smaller nowadays). There are many great Proverbs that can cover these types of friendships. One of my favorites is, "Hatred stirs up conflict, but love covers over all wrongs" (Proverbs 10:12). Well, there we go. We cannot be hateful or hold grudges if we claim to be Christians who always love. It makes us no better than others, if not worse. We must forgive as we are forgiven by Christ.

Did you know Jesus's friends hurt *Him*? When *He* needed them the most, *His* disciples let *Him* down. In Matthew Jesus explains to *His* friends what *He* needs of them: "...'My soul is overwhelmed with sorrow to the point of death. Stay here and keep watch with me'" (26:38). However, they could not do as *He* asked. They fell asleep three times, letting *Him* down. It seems a simple request from the Lord, but they failed *Him*. I bet you have felt failed by friends; I know I have. I have not asked for anything, and maybe that is my error, but I expected those who were my friends to watch over me, check on me, and be by my side when I felt sorrow. Judas, one of Jesus's twelve chosen disciples, turned against *Him* in a deadly way. Jesus knew this was coming. John replays for us what Jesus said the night of the last supper. "...Very truly I tell you, one of you is going to betray me" (John 13:21). And sure enough, Judas betrays Jesus to a crowd of people carrying weapons by identifying *Him* with a kiss, the kiss of death. The last story I want to share is probably the most hurtful one in my eyes. Again, in Matthew we are told after the events of the Last Supper that Jesus predicted Peter would deny or disown *Him*, not once but three times. Of course, Peter says *he* would never! I bet if I told people just days before that they would deny our friendship to side with *him*, they would have said they would never as well. I do not believe people planned to hurt me or you. I believe it is just a reaction to circumstances beyond their control. And you guessed it, Peter did just as Jesus said in Matthew 26:70, 72, and 74 after Jesus's arrest. "'...I don't know what you're talking about,' *he* said to a servant girl who stated *he* had been seen with Jesus and twice yelled, 'I don't know the man!'" This all was hurtful to Jesus even though *He* knew it was coming. People are just that, people. We all make mistakes. If the disciples would hurt Jesus, then surely, we would hurt each other. Wouldn't it be nice to know who was going to betray you in advance? Well, we don't, but *He* does.

When the news hit the streets that I was getting divorced, my phone blew up! People texted and called in show of support. I do not think that was fake. I do believe everyone truly cared. More so they were shocked! Nobody saw it coming. For months I did not have a lonely day. People took me to lunch, dinner, movies, and just came by to check on me. But then it mostly stopped. I had to decipher who was truly my friend, whose life just got busy (but still cared from afar), and those who really just wanted the gossip. I began to pray and turned to the good ole faithful Bible for answers. God showed me it did not matter. I mean let's be real, I would want to know the gossip too! Inquiring minds and all. "Whoever would foster love covers over an offense, but whoever repeats the matter separates close friends" (Proverbs 17:9). Regardless of the original intent, I am going with life just got busy. I mean it happens to us all, right? The same thing happens when people get married, have babies, or have a death in the family. You are flooded with support at first, then it dwindles off. I am guilty of it myself. It does not mean they are no longer friends, just maybe not your BFF, ya know? Trust me, you will know the difference.

James, Jesus's brother, encourages us to be "quick to listen, but slow to speak and slow to become angry, because human anger does not produce the righteousness that God desires" (James 1:19–20). This is difficult I know; we are just sinners after all. The Bible refers to the dangers of a loose tongue multiple times. We feel a certain way and want to react appropriately, but "the mouth speaks what the heart is full of" (Matthew 12:34). EEKS! If you simmer on that for a minute, you may realize you are guilty, as I am, of that happening. Proverbs 10:19 reminds us, "When there are many words, transgression is unavoidable, but *he* who restrains *his* lips is wise." I admit I get angry and am nowhere near slow in the area of speaking. And man, that tongue of mine can be fierce! However, these are areas I am working on. Maybe if this is true of you as well, we can work on them together. Let's try to be slow to react when we feel hurt by *them*.

I also had those friends who I say, "my husband got in the divorce." I was hurt and angry that they obviously chose *him* and just *him*. Hello? Over here! What about poor me? And there was God, after letting me sulk in it for a while, telling me to forgive and move on. Was it *His* doing to separate you from these friendships, or was it *theirs*? Remember the free will thing? The decision to stop (or never start) reaching out to me or to choose *him* instead of me was conscious on *their* parts. But let's look at it from their point of view. Being in the middle of anyone's divorce is not fun. Either you love them both and feel stuck to choose between caramel or butterscotch (two of my favs), or you lean toward one of them more due to history, common interests, and personality. The ones who feel really stuck in the middle tend to just fade off and become acquaintances or better yet "old friends" with both. The others' pendulums obviously swing to one side. I have some fans on my side of the field too (gotta love a sports analogy)! These friends, let me tell you, are fiercely on my side. They see, hear, and feel my suffering, and *he* would probably not want to run into one of them out in public. These ladies would go crazy on *him*, and though I do not condone it from a Christian stand-point, I sure do love *them* for having my back always. Anyway, let's try to get over the hurt from the loss of some of *them* and move on. We have many, many new friendships in our future and some refurbished old friendships. Most importantly we have relationships to look forward to with people God has purposely put on our team.

He may have purposely taken some of the people out of my life; after all *He* hears things we do not and sees things we cannot. However, *He* replaces *them* with who I need in the now. Some old friends stepped up to show support, and some new strong friendships emerged out of the darkness. Proverbs has a verse that really hit home when I lost some relationships. "One who has unreliable friends soon comes to ruin, but there is a friend who sticks closer than a broth-er" (Proverbs 18:24). Do you have one of these? It really only takes one. I do and boy do I love her! She has become more of a little sister than a friend over the years. Actually, more are developing. All I need to do is have a few conversations with people to determine if they are the kind of friends I want, better yet, need in my life. Proverbs again tells us about the right kind of relationships we should have in 13:20: "Walk with the wise and become wise, for a companion of fools suffers harm." I am just gonna leave that right there and let you mull over it. It is deep, right? Paul speaks of this when writing to the people of the Corinthian church. It is explained that we should not be misled because "...bad company corrupts good character" (1 Corinthians 15:33). You know those friends. You may love *them*, and you should (*His* commandment and all), but are *they* good examples for you? Are *they* really who you should be hanging around with daily or every weekend? Do *they* make you a better person? Are you using your free will to make poor decisions when with *them*? If after being with *them* you feel guilt or regret almost every time, then maybe it is time for some changes.

So how do you know when it is right? You know the saying, "it should be easy"? I disagree to an extent. When you are together, it should be an easy, no stress, relaxing, trusting relationship. But like all relationships, friendship takes work. Ever get frustrated when you are the only one who plans, calls, and texts, or are you the friend that never reaches out in return? Friendship should be based on a love and mutual respect of each other. I know we all get busy and forgetful, but that excuse cannot last forever. Also, as a person who struggles with anxiety, I know that it can be difficult to be the one who reaches out first. I make myself. I have a system. It helps me not forget people. Texting is my preferred method; it seems this is becoming most people's these days. Texting is allowing us to be social without being social, but it is better than nothing. It can at least be an icebreaker. You can also call and actually talk (insert gasp). I do this for my mom who needs to hear my voice daily. I also do this when no response from a friend via text after a few attempts. You can even send a letter the old-fashioned way. People love to get mail! A few friends have dropped off gifts or sent notes to me through the actual United States Postal Service, and it brings the biggest smile to my face (the Amazon surprises are nice too)! When I do get a chance to go to dinner or watch a movie with my true friends, it is easy. I leave with my emotional tank filled and hopefully filled up *theirs* as well. It is worth every drop of effort!

Who has hurt you? How? Can you see their dilemma? Can you get to a place where you can forgive them? Guess what I think you should do? Write about it! Oh, and pray:

> Oh Lord my God, loss in any form is painful. Please heal me from the hurt caused by others. Forgive me for being angry or hateful due to *their* reactions to my situation. Help me see it is not an easy place to be for anyone. Teach me to forgive and move forward whether it is *Your* will they remain in my life or not. I pray *You* put friendships, new and old, in my life that bring me joy and hope. Introduce me to those who show me undying love and support and guide me to be that kind of friend in return. In *Your* wonderful name I pray. Amen.

BE A JOURNALER!

BE A JOURNALER!

_____

_____

_____

_____

_____

_____

_____

_____

_____

_____

_____

_____

_____

_____

_____

_____

_____

_____

_____

_____

_____

_____

_____

_____

_____

_____

Him

PART TWO:

Him

I am thrilled to write about my God! Just getting to this part of the book has made me giddy inside. I have learned a great deal about *His* undying love for me in my forty-plus years. I was raised to know the almighty God and the love and sacrifice *His* son made by dying on the cross for me and my sins. As with many children raised in the church, the first verse I memorized was John 3:16: "For God so loved the world that he gave his one and only Son, that whoever believes in him shall not perish but have eternal life." I am not sure if it is because I am older, because I am wiser, or because I am in so much pain, but that verse has become clearer than ever. Maybe it's a combination of them all. I cannot even imagine sacrificing my son for others' benefits! That is a sacrifice and love that is almost impossible to comprehend. I say almost because if you study your Bible, you will see that *His* selfless love and dedication is seen throughout, and that if you know what to look for in your own life, you can see it there as well.

This part of the book is meant to shed some light on some questions I had that you too might be having about God and *His* role in our pain. I will discuss blame, that freewill thing in more detail, faith, and God's will for you. I hope to encourage you to pray and study the word of God and to show you examples of *His* amazing forgiveness and love.

Did I mention I am way type A, a control freak, a real-life, diagnosed person with obsessive compulsive disorder? Many people say they have OCD, and many people can have attributes of it, but one who truly has it struggles with mundane daily tasks. I have definitely gotten better and have been on and off medications for it for twenty years, though many people in my life (especially my STBX) would probably say it is still going strong within me. It is difficult to let go of control because certain things need to be a certain way for my world to feel balanced. It is not about other people and them being sloppy or unorganized, it is about what I need to do, see, and have in order to feel safe and relaxed. This is very difficult for most people to comprehend as it is common for people to not be able to truly understand others with mental illnesses or any difference for that matter. It is not easy to be my friend, coworker, child, or spouse. However, with a little knowledge about my disorder, you can find that it isn't too hard to figure out my needs (or quirks) and enjoy my company. I mean, I am a pretty fun girl! Anyway, you can see how all this divorce stuff may have sent me into a severe depression. I had no control over my life. I felt like I was falling, flailing the entire way down. I thought that *he* controlled the situation, the outcome of my life and future. I was wrong, *He* does! Funny how after all these years, this terrible, horrible situation has made me truly stronger in every way, even with my disorder. Thanks to *Him* I am now a recovering perfectionist. I have learned to let go and let God. It wasn't (and still isn't) easy; I had to be broken down and built back up, but I am slowly becoming a better me. As I sit here typing, there are clothes lying over the banister, puzzle pieces all over the table, and actual "stuff" lying on my kitchen counter. What? Who have I become? These things would usually eat me up inside.

Anxiety is real for many people; some are diagnosed, but most are not. Anxiety is an overwhelming feeling of helplessness, fear, worry, lack of control, indecisiveness, loneliness, or all these negative emotions jumbled together. Worry is not new to the world, though it is heightened with the existence of technology: media (especially social media), television, airbrushed magazine covers, filtered pictures, video games, and apps. We have to realize that all these negative feelings do not come from God. Instead, *He* gives us ways of fighting them off and overcoming them. In 2 Timothy 1:7 Paul writes to Timothy, "For God has not given us a spirit of fear, but of power and of love and of a sound mind" (NKJV). Paul also writes to the Christians of Philippi, "Do not be anxious about anything, but in every situation, by prayer and petition, with thanksgiving, present your requests to God. And the peace of God, which transcends all understanding, will guard your hearts and your minds in Jesus Christ" (Philippines 4:6–7). Let me break it down for you; when you feel anxious, give it to God. This is a feeling from Satan and heightened by the world in which we live. Letting go of it is an ultimate display of trust in *Him*. I know it is not easy. It takes time, practice, and prayer. I fail, trust me, I fail, but *He* forgives me and rightens me. Throw yourself into *His* word and surround yourself with *His* people. It makes an amazing difference, you'll see.

I did not know it would happen, but as the months pass as I am writing this book, I am feeling and seeing myself grow and change for the stronger. And that is just the beginning of *His* part in this. *He* knew this storm was coming, and *He* has had me the whole time. Always did, always will. So why then, if *He* knew it was coming, did *He* not stop it? Let's pray about it.

Gracious God, *You* know my past, my present, and have seen my future. Help me to understand that *You* are not to blame, but *You* are to be glorified for *Your* undying love and support through the messy times in my life. Teach me when to decipher when things are because of *him* and when they are because of *You*. Guide me in forgiveness, strengthen my faith, and give me hope for the future. In *Your* visionary name. Amen.

PART 2-1:

The Blame Game

I know many of you cried out. "Why God?" "Why me, Lord?" Maybe even worse, not so nice words when you were on your knees. I was in my closet, that was my habitual, break-down, safe spot. You know that movie that says you should use your closet as a room to pray, to fight wars against evil? I was using mine to fight God, and I did not even realize it. I begged *Him* to make it stop. I questioned *Him* on the daily. In times of trial, we often look for someone to blame, and *He* is an easy target. In Romans 9:20 Paul questions the Gentiles and Jews, "But who are you, a human being, to talk back to God? "Shall what is formed say to the one who formed it, 'Why did you make me like this?'" Pretty nervy of us to question *Him*, huh? So why do we? Out of fear, lack of knowledge, foolishness, and in my case, because I knew *He* could take it.

Blame started all the way back in Genesis in the Garden of Eden. Remember earlier when I talked about Satan's interjection into our relationships and the first sin? Guess who Adam blamed for feasting on the forbidden fruit? Eve! Yep, just like a man to blame the woman (funny but, I know, not nice). But *he* takes the blame even further by turning it on God. "The man said, 'The woman you put here with me—she gave me some fruit from the tree, and I ate it.'" Adam basically says to God it was *His* fault for making her because she was the one who made *him* eat it. But let's be real, she didn't have to twist *his* arm too hard. She offered; *he* took. *he* did not question her or try to talk her out of it. I can poke a little fun at man, though, because what woman did was pretty bad too. Eve blamed the serpent, but in doing so, she showed her trust in the devil and disbelief of God's word. She fell prey to Satan's trickery. After all the devil is very smart. We probably all know that firsthand. So why would God even tempt them with that tree? Why even put it in there and say you cannot partake of its yumminess? And there begins the first questioning of God, *His* will, *His* purpose, and *His* plan. Adam and Eve are responsible for the first sin on record. And yes, they were disciplined by the Father. They immediately recognized their nakedness and were embarrassed. So, they are who you can thank for having to wear all those uncomfortable clothes today. They were booted out of the Garden of Eden, left to hunt, and plant their own food. Eve, being the first to sin and to tempt Adam, was given the pain of childbirth, which included the overwhelming joy of menstruation (read that sarcastically, of course). Wow! What a turn of events because of sin. They forfeited their perfect life. I wish all couples were mandated to read and intensely study Adam and Eve's story before marriage. It is a model of what NOT to do! Adam and Eve created the first nuclear family, meaning a couple and their dependent family, the core. Adam and Eve were role models for their children, as all parents are. These common people were not happy with what they had. They wanted more. They wanted to be God's equals, they wanted answers and knowledge of things they were not privy to. They were tempted by power and desire. Know how that affected their children? Well, their son Cain killed his younger brother Abel out of jealousy of God's acceptance.

Apple doesn't fall far and all. Do you know there is no good and perfect example of a nuclear family in the Bible? That is because marriage, children, and family are messy. Somewhere in the lineage, someone or even all of them lost their way and were driven by outside, evil factors. Doesn't this all still happen today? Do money, people, work, and other countless things keep us from going to church, praying, or reading our Bibles? Does jealousy affect our motivations? Why yes, yes it does.

In Mark 7 we are told a story about how the Pharisees and some of the teachers of the law gathered near Jesus and his disciples and began to question why they did not follow the laws. In this particular story, the disciples were eating with uncleaned hands. The law stated that you must wash your hands in a ceremonial way before eating food with your hands. However, Jesus answered that the Pharisees, lawmakers, and those following *their* rules were hypocrites in Mark 7:6–8:

> These people honor me with their lips, but their hearts are far from me. They worship me in vain; their teachings are merely human rules. You have let go of the commands of God and are holding on to human traditions.

I for one am totally called out on this one. I am guilty of always honoring *Him* with my lips but not always my actions. I have allowed the human traditions, my non-Christian and Christian friends, my spouse, social media, and my own selfishness to cause me to worship *Him* in vain. We have to see the errors in our ways. We have to first take responsibility for our faults and actually be willing to change. Our Lord further explained in Mark that the hands being "cleaned" was not defiling their bodies because it is not what we put into our body that defiles us but what comes out of it. Think on that!

I have felt like I am losing a great deal all at once, but I know *He* would never leave me. Psalm 94:14 is just one of the many places in the Bible that reiterates that fact by stating, "For the Lord will not reject his people: he will never forsake his inheritance." God has proven time and time again with Gentiles and Jews, the wicked and the saints alike that even in the darkest hours, *He* will show. This Psalm is a prayer for God's rules to be spelled out. However, if you keep reading through the Psalms, you will find that God's love is not a get out of jail free card. *He* allows things to happen to bring us to our knees, to bring us closer to *Him* and to salvation. Also, Psalms reminds us that we will be judged by our Heavenly Father. *He* is our parent after all. Maybe you can relate to this. If you are a parent, you know children need discipline. They have an innate desire for consequences for their actions, even though they probably do not realize it. That is why they test us. That is why when no consequences are given for their actions, they stray even farther and act out even worse. Parents do not enjoy punishing their children, just as God does not enjoy punishing us. Well OK, at times it might feel a bit good to ground a kid who is back talking or who consistently breaks curfew, but you understand what I am saying, right? When God's people do not follow the rules or commandments and become even farther from *Him* and *His* word, then *He* does punish.

There are multiple stories in the Bible about discipline by the Father. In the book of Numbers, we are told how Moses and the Israelites aimlessly wandered the vast wilderness for forty years for disobeying God's command to attack and take their land. They did not have faith in God and questioned *His* plan. Later in 2 Samuel, David and Bathsheba's firstborn child died due to David's adulterous and murderous ways.

Jeremiah tells of the exile of the Jews from Babylon due to their unfaithfulness to God. *He* compares them to an unfaithful wife and rebellious children. The Lord said to Jeremiah, "...I warned them again and again, saying, 'Obey me'. But they did not listen or pay attention; instead, they followed the stubbornness of their evil hearts" (Jeremiah 11:7–8). To backtrack, God made a promise to the people of Israel that *He* would bring them to safety, out of hot, miserable Egypt. But they would also have to promise to follow *His* rules. Well, they did not hold up their end of the bargain. They began to create and worship false gods and idols. They denied the God who saved them. So yes, *He* punished them. In Jeremiah 11:11–12 God states, "...I will bring on them a disaster they cannot escape. Although they cry out to me, I will not listen to them." Sounds harsh, right? These verses of the Bible are often misunderstood by nonbelievers and believers alike. This is often true of many verses in the Bible when not read in full context. You see God never meant for them to stay unhappy or in harm's way, *He* just wanted to bring them back to their knees. *He* wanted to show them that the false gods they were worshipping could not save them, only *He* could. Isn't that the job of a parent? Later in Jeremiah, God makes a statement that shows us *His* deep love for *His* people. "'For I know the plans I have for you,' declares the Lord, 'plans to prosper you and not harm you, plans to give you hope and a future'" (29:11). You have probably heard that one before; it is one of the most quoted verses of the Bible. But did you know it in context to the story above? This was what *He* told Jeremiah to tell the exiled people *He* had taken from Jerusalem to Babylon. This was their second chance. What an awesome father we have in God!

However, time after time *His* people failed *Him*. Soon *He* realized man could not refrain from sin and follow the first covenant (rules) set by *Him*. This is why *He* sent *His* son. You see, God did not make Adam and Eve, the Pharisees and law-makers, or the Jews of Babylon sin; *He* even warned them what not to do in order to continue their happy, peaceful, sin-less lives. However, they made the choice (FREE WILL). They sinned; they sealed their fate. When somebody does something bad to you, think, did God do it, or did *he/she*? God may have allowed it to happen and even knew it was going to, but it does not mean *He* chose it. As mentioned earlier, you must look at your own life and decide if you were perhaps in need of some discipline from your father. Were you heading in the wrong direction? Were you idolizing false Gods or refusing to listen to God's commands? It may be difficult but be vulner-able and write about it. In my case it was both things above. God did not choose to make my STBX leave, *he* made that aw-ful decision, and *he* will have to live with the consequences and deal with God's discipline. It is not for me to punish *him*; I am not *his* parent. Think on that when trying to keep your children from *him* or any of the other million ways you have or have wished to punish an ex. It is not your place, though I know you think it will make you feel better, it will not (well, at least it would not for very long). My married life took a turn I did not like years ago, but I continued in it anyway. I was mov-ing farther from God in my marriage, and I hated it but didn't have the strength to change it. I tried here and there to start a Bible study, go to church regularly, join a small group, stay away from those who negatively influenced me, but mostly I failed. I do not feel God punished me with the divorce. I do know that *He* has used this bad situation to right me, though. Remember, *He* does not want us to sin against *Him* or hurt each other, but that has not stopped anyone from doing it since the days of Adam and Eve. Lucky for us, we can be for-given if we just pray.

God our Father, it is oftentimes too easy to blame *You* when things go wrong in my life. Father, help me to discern when these things are happening because of man or because of *You*. Guide me in righting my life when *You* know I have fallen off the path *You* have laid for me. Help me to understand when *You* are disciplining me out of love and to better my future. Please keep me from taking revenge on others as it is not my job to discipline *Your* children. Thank *You*, Heavenly Father, for loving me enough to want to give me guidance and correct my errors. Thank *You* for not giving up on me when I am at my worst. Thank *You* for forgiving me when I humble myself by admitting the errors of my ways and sincerely ask! In *Your* parental name I pray. Amen.

BE A JOURNALER!

_____

_____

_____

_____

_____

_____

_____

_____

_____

_____

_____

_____

_____

_____

_____

_____

_____

_____

_____

_____

_____

BE A JOURNALER!

PART 2-2:

Humble Me

I am forgiven! Praise God for that because I am a sinner, girl, believe me I have some whoppers! One of the most difficult things for me has been forgiving myself for these acts against God. I literally still prayed for forgiveness for things I did as a teenager well into my thirties. I only have recently learned that by doing so I was not trusting in God. Apparently, this is a common theme among women. We tend to struggle with guilt and shame and do not forgive ourselves, so we feel unforgiven by God. So let me be clear: I AM FORGIVEN. I know this because I am a Christian. I asked Jesus Christ into my heart many years ago, and I have prayed for forgiveness by confessing my sins. I AM FORGIVEN. I cannot speak for you, but I can assure you that "if we confess our sins, he is faithful and just and will forgive us our sins and purify us from all unrighteousness" (1 John 1:9). 1 John also tells us in verse 1:10 that "if we claim we have not sinned, we make him out to be a liar and his word is not in us." I feel this is just as true if we ask for forgiveness over and over and over again for the same infraction. Now I am not speaking of doing the same sin multiple times. If you lie, ask for forgiveness, but if you lie again and then again and not ask for forgiveness, that is a problem. You have to fess up to each individual sin not because *He* did not know you did it but to show you do and that you have regret. However, if you confess, ask for forgiveness, but keep doing it over and over again, you have to look inside yourself and think: do you really feel regret? Do you really want to change? Are you truly searching for God's help and listening to *Him*? Do you really feel guilty?

Let's chat about this guilt thing. Feeling guilt is a good thing. It means you recognize the errors in your way; you are being convicted by the Holy Spirit. These feelings are what can, and hopefully will, bring you to ask for forgiveness. And then remember that "'He himself bore our sins' in his body on the cross, so that we might die to sins and live for righteousness; 'by his wounds you have been healed'" (1 Peter 2:24). Repent and believe you are forgiven. Shame has no place in your life. Shame and guilt are not the same thing. Shame is from the devil. Shame is what keeps us from feeling unforgiven. The master manipulator wants us to hold on to the sin and feel unforgiven because it makes us go against *His* word and promise. Be strong in your faith, believe God has forgiven you, and be grateful that Jesus allowed this to happen by dying for your sin on the cross. Do not let *His* death be in vain. Allow him to take away the guilt and do not feel shame any longer, that only gives the devil power. You are not alone. You are not the only sinner. "...for all have sinned and fall short of the glory of God" (Romans 3:23). We are all the same and can all be forgiven.

How does this all tie into this book? I definitely sinned in my marriage. I did not always put God first as mentioned earlier. My priorities were out of whack. Also, I allowed myself to be pulled into situations that I knew would lead to sinful acts. Should my marriage have ended because of this? No. Did it end because of this? Still, I think no. That brings us back to the whole *his* freewill thing. However, did it affect my marriage? Yes! And how I deal with the guilt now will affect my future. I have chosen to forgive myself as God has forgiven me. How you ask did I finally, after all these years, do this? Vulnerability and faith! Being vulnerable is more difficult for me than having faith. Being vulnerable means admitting your transgressions to yourself, to others, and to God. It means being open, painfully honest, and willing to change and grow. Of course, this is difficult, who wants to say, "My bad, I was wrong"? Not many of us. This makes us feel weak and exposed. We are afraid we will be judged and criticized, even laughed at by others. Oh, but, my dear friends, it is just the opposite. My vulnerability has brought people to my side. Many have reached out and thanked me for my honesty. Some have related to my stories and given me advice or even asked for my advice. My advice? Who am I to give advice? God showed me that I am the newly vulnerable person who has faith in God and that is why I should give advice. "My grace is sufficient for you, for my power is made perfect in weakness" (2 Corinthians 12:9).

One piece of advice I give is to forgive. Boy oh boy, it isn't easy! The forgiveness comes from God for sure. First and foremost, forgive yourself but then forgive others. Forgiving the *thems* in my life stunk! I wanted to hold a grudge forever, but it was eating me inside. I forgave, but I will never forget the hurt and disappointment. I think that is all right, though, because it helped mold me into who I am today. In Colossians, we again find Paul writing a letter to a church with the help of his friend Timothy. They were reaching out to the Christian people of Colossae because Paul had received word that they were being led by false teachers. The letter, which is the New Testament's twelfth book of the Bible, is again explaining how a Christian should live while on earth and a recap of the superiority of the Son of God. In Colossians 3:8, the Christians are told to "...rid yourselves of all such things as these: anger, rage, malice, slander, and filthy language from your lips." A few verses later, Paul continues:

> Therefore, as God's chosen people, holy and dearly loved, clothe yourself with compassion, kindness, humility, gentleness, and patience. Bear with each other and forgive one another if any of you has a grievance against someone. Forgive as the Lord forgave you. And over all these virtues put on love, which binds them all together in perfect unity. (Colossians 3:12-14)

Less than a year in and I have already looked *him* in the eyes and said, "I forgive you." This took a massive amount of courage, strength, and humility. *his* response was that *he* wasn't asking for my forgiveness. I feel it is because *he* was not or is not in a good place with *himself* and God, a place to receive forgiveness. but that is OK. I did what I needed to do in order to move on. *he* is not mine to fix, *he* belongs to the Father. I also told *him* multiple times I was sorry for my part in our marriage failing. At first it was a way of trying to keep him. Crying "I am sorry" over and over again and not really sure why. As I settled down a bit, months later, and truly reflected on God's word and my part in this whole sordid mess, I was able to say once, and only once, "I am sorry" and truly mean it. I have not gotten that back from *him* yet, and I may never, but again that is not for me to worry about. Don't get me wrong, I still pray for *him*. I mean I do still love *him*, and *he* will always be the father of my children. However, I cannot do much more than pray besides have faith in God's will.

Faith. "Having faith" is said by people all the time. There are tattoos, wall art, key chains, and hashtags about it all over the place. However, actually having it is much more difficult than saying you have it. You know the saying, "God won't give you more than you can handle"? That is not biblical! I learned that the hard way. During the beginning of my marital struggles, I cried out to God, "I can't take anymore," and then *he* left, and I cried it out again. My children were suffering, and I yelled it out again. Things continued to pile up on me. Job changes, struggles with selling my home, and a lengthy and stressful divorce process, and still I prayed, "I CAN'T HANDLE ANYMORE!" By the time the treacherous coronavirus of 2020 had rolled around, and we were under quarantine, I had learned my lesson. Stop telling God what I can and can't handle! If I give it all to *Him* and truly have faith by being still and knowing *He* will see me through, then it doesn't matter what comes next. It isn't always easy to have faith, I get it. Faith means not always having the answers or seeing your future. Even those standing beside Christ *Himself* in the Bible lacked it at times. Mark tells us a story of how Jesus calmed a mighty storm. *His* disciples were in a boat, and a ferocious storm threatened to sink the boat and drown the passengers, including Jesus. Yet the Lord slept. When *He* was awoken by the fearful disciples and questioned about their life-and-death situation, Jesus said to the water, "... 'Quiet! Be still!' Then the wind died down and it was completely calm. He said to his disciples, 'Why are you so afraid? Do you still have no faith?'" (Mark 4:39–40).

The disciples were afraid not only because of the storm, but because they still were terrified afterward at the sheer power of Jesus. They did not have a relationship with *Him* yet that would ease that fear. That I understand. I had fear, fear of everything for a long, long time. And again, I have been a Christian since childhood. The problem was not that I didn't know *Him*, but that I did not have the relationship with my Savior that allowed me to truly trust in *Him*. I thought I did, but really, I didn't. You know how I know? Because I now have that relationship with *Him*, and the fear is gone. Do I wonder?

Sure! Do I wish I had answers? Of course! But do I stress about it anymore? No! It really isn't something I can teach you to do. It truly is just a gift from God, a peace, and a reassurance of a future, even though I cannot see it. So now instead of saying, "I can't take anymore," I yell out, "Bring it on, world, my God and I got this!" Be humble but stay strong in your faith.

I have to pray for God to humble me. To make me worthy of Him and not to worry how I measure up to others or be prideful in my endeavors. "...Clothe yourselves with humility toward one another, because, 'God opposes the proud but shows favor to the humble'" (1 Peter 5:5). Even Jesus Christ *Himself* showed humility. This was one of *His* greatest attributes. The obvious time and the greatest show of humility on record in history is when *He* died on the cross. *He* had the power to ask *His* Father to end *His* suffering. Can you imagine having ultimate power yet humbling yourself to a commoner in order to save others? In a fictitious way, this reminds me of Iron Man (for those of you Marvel lovers like me). I don't want to ruin it for you but watch the *End Game*. A nonfiction example is a story of a very wealthy man named Alfred Vanderbilt. He was on a sinking ship, and his status gave him one of the few life jackets and lifeboats, but instead *he* went down with the ship, helping as many children as *he* could escape the sinking vessel safely. There are thousands of examples of martyrs and heroes who gave their lives to help others during the holocaust, the civil rights movements, 9/11, Columbine, war, and more. They all had bravery and selflessness. Not all acts of humility need to lead to death, though. Some are just small gestures that mean a great deal. Jesus modeled humility even before *His* crucifixion when *He* washed *His* disciples' feet. Did you get that? Jesus Christ, the son of God, washed other people's feet! Don't for a second think you are too good to humble yourself to help others in any situation if you are able. Helping others has really aided me in recovering from hurt. There are many ways to do this. Donate your time, money, or food. Visit a nursing home, babysit friends' kids, share your story with others, and share *His* story with others. By the way, helping others? Also, biblical. "And do not forget to do good and to share with others, for with such sacrifices God is pleased" (Hebrew 13:16). It is never too late to start. What is your gift? What are you able to give or share?

> Merciful Father, thank *You* for forgiving me. Thank *You* for sending *Your* Son to model humility the day *He* died on the cross for my sins. Help me, Lord, to not only forgive myself but to let go of shame and to trust in *Your* forgiveness. Teach me to forgive as *You* have and reveal my gifts so that I may help others. Show me how having ultimate faith in *You* and *Your* plan will only bring me happiness and peace. Faithfully I pray. Amen.

BE A JOURNALER!

BE A JOURNALER!

_____

_____

_____

_____

_____

_____

_____

_____

_____

_____

_____

_____

_____

_____

_____

_____

_____

_____

_____

_____

_____

_____

_____

_____

PART 2-3:

Symbols, Symbols Everywhere

was at summer camp with an awesome bunch of church group kids from Bluff Park Baptist Church when I accepted Jesus Christ as my Lord and Savior. One of the most influential men in my entire life was my pastor at the time. Brother John sat me next to *him* and showed me *his* wedding ring. *he* asked me what it meant. "Duh, obviously that you are married." Then *he* took it off and asked me what that meant. My eyes got big, and I exclaimed, "Oh, I am telling Ms. Linda!" I just knew it meant *he* was no longer married. Can you guess *his* point? Symbolism. The ring was a symbol of *his* marriage and love. When *he* removed it, it DID NOT mean *he* was no longer married as little naïve Kristina had thought. Now that I am older, I see that even when I am lost, sinning, lacking in faith, not in church or studying my Bible, God still loves me and is dedicated to me and to you. I have recently realized that the love we are told about in Corinthians, the undying love that I felt I did not have and would no longer find has always been there and always will. It comes from God. I was devastated to think that the man I thought *He* had chosen for me, to protect me, love me, honor me no matter what was no longer by my side. I was broken that the friends who had my back, cared for me and my children, and were there all the time were now gone. Now what? Let's talk about symbolism, prayer, studying our Bible, and the promise of God's love a little bit more.

My son was upset one day because the cross *he* wore daily around *his* neck was lost. I get it; it was important to *him* and made *him* feel like *he* was protected. Insert lecture from Mom on symbolism. I explained that it was OK to want to wear it as a testament of *his* faith but that more importantly *his* actions and words were proof of his devotion to *Him*. Symbols are everywhere! Not just religious. Symbols of our favorite teams, animals, as well as our political and religious affiliations are worn on our clothing, printed on our skin, and stuck to our bumpers. However, it is important to not idolize the symbol or misinterpret what it stands for. Common religious symbols are the cross, dove, star, angel, and even the Bible. These items can be reminders to us of our faith and used to display our faith to others as well. However, living the life is the ultimate testimony. Christians themselves are symbols of God's love and promise if we in fact are living our lives right (or at least trying super-duper hard). Many people believe *He* sends us symbols or signs to guide our lives or as reminders. The Bible concurs, saying, "God also testified to it by signs, wonders and various miracles, and by gifts of the Holy Spirit distributed by his will"(Hebrews 2:4). Let me be clear, though, these symbols are not our loved ones reincarnated! It does not work that way my friends.

My family has always felt the common symbol of the cardinal was a reminder of our grandmother and the uncommon symbol of the ladybug was for my grandfather. You would think the opposite, I know, but Grandma loved birds. Once she babysat my pet birds for me. She wanted to give them some fresh air and sunshine, so she took the cage outside to hang on the porch. Bet you know what's coming. She was devastated when she dropped the cage and let them fly away. However, she freed them, and we often thought we heard them chirping in the trees nearby. The family actually joked about it for years at my poor grandma's expense.

Once I went to visit Grandpa in the hospital. It was a cold, snowy winter day in Akron, Ohio. I was scared of losing *him*. My grandpa was the Christian leader of our family. *he* was a true man of God. *he* portrayed that undying, all-forgiving love for *his* family. *he* was the Godly husband that all women dreamed off. The love my grandparents had was the kind you see in the movies. On that wintry day, in the hospital room, as we prayed to God for *his* health and selfishly our wish for *him* to be all right, ladybugs crawled up the arm of his hospital bed. Talk about a sign! By the grace of God, Grandpa was OK that trip but passed away shortly after. So now every time I see a ladybug, I of course think of *him*. It gives me reassurance that God is thinking of me. It is almost *His* way of saying, "WWGD, What Would Grandpa Do"?

You see, symbols are signs from the Holy Spirit. The Holy Spirit is one of the three Trinity. God the Father, Jesus Christ the Son, and the Holy Spirit. Luke wrote in Acts that Peter told a massive crowd of Jews about the Christian way of life. When they inquired what they should do in order to change their ways, "Peter replied, 'Repent and be baptized, every one of you, in the name of Jesus Christ for the forgiveness of your sins. And you will receive the gift of the Holy Spirit'"(Acts 2:39). Jesus promises us the Holy Spirit in the book of John saying:

> If you love me, keep my commands. And I will ask the Father, and *He* will give you another advocate to help you and be with you forever-the

Spirit of truth. The world cannot accept him, because it neither sees him nor knows him. But you know him, for he lives with you and will be in you. (14:15–17)

Remember me talking about signs at the beginning of this book? Those came from the Holy Spirit. Remember me talking about guilt? Again, from the Holy Spirit. As I have written this book, the perfect verses have come to me, sometimes while studying my Bible, sometimes through friends or family, and sometimes from social media. How did I know which ones to use to encourage and teach you? Yep, you guessed it, Holy Spirit! Here's the thing with it, though: you have to be willing to accept the Holy Spirit's guidance. You have to open yourself up by being vulnerable and having faith. Amazing how it all comes together, huh? So how does one achieve this openness? Prayer, of course.

Oh, the power of prayer. It seems such a simple task. Close your eyes, bow your head, and talk. However, the words tend to escape us. Have you heard preachers, deacons, and religious leaders pray? It is so elegant and biblical sounding. It makes us feel that our prayers are ignorant or not worthy enough for the Lord. This is not so! Again, enter the Holy Spirit. "...The Spirit helps us in our weakness. We do not know what we ought to pray for, but the Spirit himself intercedes for us though wordless groans" (Romans 8:26). First off, God knows our needs. If the words escape you, just sit in quiet with *Him*; *He* will hear your heart. Second, instead of thinking you need to regurgitate some fancy words of a prayer you heard before or stressing about the worthiness of your prayer, just talk to *Him*. Speak to *Him* like you are talking to a friend. Also, in the book of John, which by the way is one of the four Gospels (which are the written accounts of Jesus's life and teachings), Jesus calls us friends. "You are my friends if you do what I command" (John 15:14). If you pray to *Him* as you speak to a loving friend, the words will come. Also, practice makes, well not perfection (*He* isn't looking for that), but it definitely gets easier. I know it is especially difficult to pray aloud in front of others, which is not a required act of a Christian by the way. In Matthew 6:6 we are told that "... when you pray. Go into your room, close the door, and pray to your Father, who is unseen. Then your Father, who sees what is done in secret, will reward you." However, if you want to get more comfortable praying in front of others, practice by praying aloud alone. I do this in the car, walking through the house, in bed, really anywhere I can. Also, at dinner, me and my boys rotate saying the prayer. This helps me model praying for them and gives them experience praying aloud. I want them to feel comfortable praying. It is so, so important to pray. When you are lonely, scared, confused, guilty, or regretful, pray. But also, do not forget to pray when you are happy, relieved, surprised, and grateful. "Pray continually, give thanks in all circumstances; for this is God's will for you in Christ Jesus" (1 Thessalonians 5:17–18).

There are countless verses in the Bible about prayer and faith. But what I want to bring to your attention is a story. A story I sort of relate to and probably you will as well. There is this man in the Old Testament named Job. Also, as a side note if you were not aware, the first thirty-nine books of the Bible that come prior to the Gospels are considered the Old Testament, happening before the presence of Jesus Christ on the Earth. Anyway, Job was a righteous, God-loving, God-fearing man. *he* was tremendously blessed with family, friends, wealth, and happiness. Job was a great parent. Every morning *he* offered up burnt offerings in the name of his ten children in case they have sinned against *Him*. Satan comes along one day and says to God that this holy man on Earth was only so because *he* was happy, protected, and majorly blessed by God. The devil challenges God by saying, "...now stretch out your hand and strike everything he has, and he will surely curse you to your face" (Job 1:11). God allows Job to be tested. *He* tells Satan to do his worse "... but on the man himself do not lay a finger" (Job 1:12). Then the havoc starts. Job is tested to the fullest extent of evil. Bet you know that feeling! *he* lost his livestock and many servants due to multiple attacks and invasions and a fire that fell from the sky. Job was cursed with painful, flesh-eating sores all over *his* body, and worst of all, *he* lost his home and all *his* children in a devastating windstorm. Man, that Satan is vile! The devil will do anything and everything to get us to turn from our God. This rings true even today. I have lost so much in the last year, but nothing compared to Job. I make myself remember that on the really dark days. I have my amazing children, a roof over my head (though I have to give that up soon), and family and friends that care about me. Try! Try, try, try to be grateful for all that you do have.

Remember, it can always get worse. Do you think Job was grateful? Do you think *he* cursed God? *his* wife actually encouraged *him* to do so, saying, "...Curse God and die!" (Job 2:9). She hated to see her husband suffer and questioned why *he* would continue to have faith in *Him*. Job replied to her, "... Shall we accept good from God, and not trouble?" (Job 2:10). *he* believed, "...The LORD gave and the LORD has taken away; may the name of the LORD be praised" (Job 1:20).

I know what you are thinking. I am not this perfect! I struggle to be grateful and not question God when things are really bad. Job did question God, though, by cursing the day *he* was born. Wondering why *he* just didn't die at birth. Job Chapter 3 contains twenty-six verses of *him* questioning and wondering and spiraling down the rabbit hole of doubt. Then came Job's friends. Three friends to sit by *his* side to listen, empathize, and offer advice. This is what true friendship looks like people! Just be there when someone is in need. You should not have to be asked, just show up! One friend, Eliphaz, guides him by stating, "You will pray to him, and he will hear you, and you will fulfill your vows" (Job 22:27). Great advice! Sadly, they also spoke ignorance. They assumed (you know what they say about assuming) and repeatedly told Job *his* suffering was due to sin, and *he* must repent. Prior to *his* doubt, there was not sin. This was not why all this mayhem was happening to *him*. Although *his* friends being there was supportive, *he* realized *he* could only get true answers from God. When doing so, God reminds Job of *His* authority, power over all, wisdom, and understanding. Job then blessed God by repenting and stating, "I know you can do all things; no purpose of yours can be thwarted" (Job 42:2). Know what thwarted means? Me neither, I had to look it up. It means prevented from doing something. God's purpose cannot be prevented, opposed, or stopped because *He* is the Almighty. I could really dig deep into this story, but maybe I will save that for a future book. However, I will let you off the hook now and tell you that there was a happy ending. God rewarded Job for *his* statement of faith. *he* questioned things but, in the end, prayed to God with humility, vulnerability, and trust. Guess what God did? Blessed *him*! First, the Lord God got angry with Job's friends for not speaking the truth about God. Lesson learned: be a supportive friend but do not speak of things you have no knowledge of. "After Job had prayed for his friends, the LORD restored his fortunes and gave him twice as much as he had before" (Job 42:10). I am not saying my trials nor yours are necessarily equivalent to Job's suffering, but I do feel connected to this story. I am suffering. I have lost. However, my faith has only gotten stronger and deeper. Being called to write this book has been my lifeline. I have stepped up my prayer game, and it is fierce! My rewards thus far have been peace and *His* love. Stay tuned for more blessings I believe will come.

I know I am loved. Even when I was broken over losing what I thought was the love of my life, I knew I had love from my God and *His* son. Jesus loves me, this I know for sure! *He* died on the cross for me as the ultimate sacrifice and show of love. Any successful relationship is a love triangle. Let's use a little symbolic visualization for this one. Imagine you and the other person as the bottom angles along the base of the triangle and Jesus Christ and the Holy Spirit being the sides leading up to the top point being God. This is perfect unity. However, if you take out one of the sides, you no longer have a triangle. You no longer have a strong pathway to God. Your base becomes weakened. The more you and the other angle, whether a spouse or a friend or even a child, strengthen the sides, the stronger your triangle will be, and the connection to God is greater. In my marriage, we allowed the relationship we had with the sides to become weak, this doesn't mean God wasn't there anymore, just that our foundation wasn't sturdy. We started pulling away from the Jesus side of our triangle and no longer hearing the Holy Spirit side. We had lost our solid ground. The good news, mathematically speaking, is you can find a missing side if you know the other two sides or the three angles (being the two people and God). Meaning you can get your relationship back on track. But what if the other angle is gone? Not God, though, *He* is always there! Here me clear, *He* will never leave you, your top angle is intact! But if a friend or spouse leaves the triangle, what happens? It is still solvable! Maybe with the same person, maybe with another, but it is repairable and can be made whole again. Your past relationships are not the Bermuda Triangle. You will not be lost forever!

Jesus uses a symbolic example in Matthew 7:24–27 during His Sermon on the Mount teaching that:

Therefore everyone who hears these words of mine and puts them into practice is like a wise man who built his house on the rock. The rain came down, the streams rose, and the winds blew and beat against that house; yet it did not fall, because it had its foundation on the rock. But everyone who hears these words of mine and does not put them into practice is like a foolish man who built his house on sand. The rain came down, the streams rose, and the winds blew and beat against that house, and it fell with a great crash.

What is your "house" built on? Is your "triangle" complete? What are you missing? Are you worshipping a symbol more than the meaning behind it? Reflect on your life and relationship with the Holy Trinity and decide what your next steps are to become a stronger, better you.

Mighty Builder, I ask for *You* to strengthen my foundation. Use symbols as a way to remind me, get my attention, and keep me grounded. Help me to not idolize symbols but to truly understand the meaning behind them. Please aid me in completing my relationship triangles to have real, meaningful, Christlike connections with others. Bless the relationships I have that are right in my life and remove the ones that are not. Help me, Mighty Father, to know and understand the difference and to love and forgive others regardless of if *they* are in my life now or not. In *Your* Divine name I pray. Amen.

BE A JOURNALER!

_____

_____

_____

_____

_____

_____

_____

_____

_____

_____

_____

_____

_____

_____

_____

_____

_____

_____

_____

_____

_____

_____

_____

BE A JOURNALER!

hymn

PART THREE:

hymn

Every morning when I wake, *he* is on my mind. It has been over a year, and I still miss *him*, wish *he* was lying beside me, and wonder what *he* is doing now. I wake up thinking things like, "Last year on this day, we were at the beach," or "Wish *he* could help me with yard work today." Silly stuff I know, but maybe you can relate. Even when I am hurt, angry, and disgusted with *him* for what *he* did to me and my kids, I still wake up thinking of *him*. Every morning after that initial shock, I pray. Pray for *Him* to come into my mind and fill me with strength and hope. In answer *He* gives me a song. Every morning when I get out of bed, *He* fills my mind and heart with lyrics. I proceed through my morning routine of getting dressed, feeding the dogs and cat, and making hot tea, singing songs of *His* promises and love. This saves me; every day the music saves me.

When you hear the word *hymn*, you probably think of opening a hardcover brown book you grabbed from the back of the wooden pew, standing in church, and singing the songs of your grandparents' days. At least I do. However, a *hymn* is any poem or song, old or new, that glorifies God. The ones that speak to me most are the newer contemporary songs I have recently learned in church and on my favorite Christian radio station. You know, the ones that hold my attention during church services when I struggle to focus my spiraling mind and emotions on anything else. The lyrics of these *hymns* bring me to tears, create an involuntary motion in my arms to lift toward Heaven, and have me belting out the words even when my voice is cracking. I do not care if those around me hear, only that God can. Well, you know what they say, "Make a joyful noise unto the Lord..." (Psalm 100:1 KJV). It has always amazed me how someone who does not know me in some unknown place far away can write and record the words that I need to hear at a given time in my life. How do they know what I am going through and understand the deep, dark secret emotions I feel? During this D word and writing journey, it dawned on me that they don't, but *He* does! This is *their* gift! The gift they are sharing with the world.

As mentioned earlier, God calls people to do things for many reasons that are not really what one would consider their forte. However, God gives each of us special gifts, and we are to use them to glorify *Him*. God uses people, most we will never even meet, to help us in our times of need. 1 Peter states that "each of you should use whatever gift you have received to serve others" (4:10). I am grateful beyond measure that music artists have chosen to use their God-given talent to glorify *His* name and speak to me (well, not just me but sometimes it feels like it).

In that letter Paul wrote to the Ephesians, *he* also explains that in order to honor God, Christians should "...be filled with the Spirit, speaking to one another with psalms, hymns, and songs from the Spirit. Sing and make music from your heart to the Lord, always giving thanks to God the Father for everything..." (Ephesians 5:18–20). The book of Psalms mentions singing out to and for God multiple times. Actually, all throughout the Bible, song is mentioned as a way of praise.

Even Jesus Christ *Himself* sang a hymn with the twelve disciples after the Last Supper and before going out to the Mount of Olives. If we are to be Christlike, shouldn't we sing songs of praise, as well? I am about to give you the opportunity to "sing to the LORD a new song, for he has done marvelous things..." (Psalm 98:1). The beautiful singer and talented songwriter Lauren Daigle began her career years ago but only recently have her songs caught my attention. It is like they have been waiting for me to need them, and I need them now. You know those songs that you feel were written for you or about you. Many of hers gave me that feeling. I will spend the next three parts sharing the words of a few of her songs and their importance to us and our continued growth and healing. It is my prayer that you download the songs, if you haven't already, and make that joyful noise while truly feeling and connecting to the words. Let's pray for that together now.

> Master of Music, I ask that you use Lauren's gift of molding *Your* words into song to encourage and strengthen my bond with *You*. Help me to be filled with your presence and undying love. Put the right song in my heart when I need it most, during the times of trials and when my mind wanders from *You*. Help this to inspire me to use my voice to honor *You* and share Your story with others. In *Your* harmonious name I pray. Amen.

BE A JOURNALER!

_____

_____

_____

_____

_____

_____

_____

_____

_____

_____

_____

_____

_____

_____

_____

_____

_____

_____

_____

_____

_____

_____

_____

_____

_____

BE A JOURNALER!

PART 3-1:

He Says

I wrote earlier about being at my lowest. Questioning everything I thought I knew about my life and myself threw me into a spiral of self-loathing, pity, and worthlessness. One of the many triggers to the twenty-plus years of memories I was not equipped to reminisce over was songs on the radio. I always listen to music in the car, but I could barely do it anymore. Songs we have danced to, songs we called "ours," songs we sang along to, songs we dedicated to our sons, and artists we had seen in concert were haunting me at every turn of the key. Advice from a friend had me tuning my radio into K-LOVE, a Christian radio station, every time I got into my car. That was when I heard Lauren Daigle's song "You Say" for the first time. I know you can relate when I say I feel like that song was written for me. It was released almost exactly a year earlier to the day I heard it. I immediately downloaded it and listened to it on repeat. The pain coming from the song was mine. It was as if I wrote it sitting on my dark, lonely closet floor.

> I keep fighting voices in my mind that say I'm not enough
> Every single lie that tells me I will never measure up

Am I more than just the sum of every high and
every low?
Remind me once again just who I am because I
need to know

These words eventually began to change my mindset. As a
Christian I am humbled by these lyrics. I am not alone. I should
know better! Most importantly the things I am saying to myself
are a lie! The voice in my head selling me these lies is Satan.
Peter, one of Jesus's apostles, writes about the suffering of
Christians in 1 Peter as part of his short letter that connects what
happens to us on Earth and how it is preparing us for Heaven. 1
Peter 5:6-9 reminds us to:

Humble yourselves, therefore, under God's
mighty hand, that he may lift you up in due time.
Cast all your anxiety on him because he cares
for you. Be alert and of sober mind. Your enemy
the devil prowls around like a roaring lion looking for someone to devour. Resist him, standing
firm in faith, because you know that the family
of believers throughout the world is undergoing
the same kind of sufferings.

Peter is speaking to you, me, and so many others. We are not
alone! All Christians go through sufferings. Did you get that word
was plural? We must be humbled in our hurt and know it is not
only us who suffers. Also, Peter brings attention the master de-
mon himself coming into our heads to make us question ourselves and our Lord. However, we must fight off the thoughts
caused by *him* and have faith that we will be delivered from our
pain in God's time.

Every high and low in my life do define me, I believe this to be true, but they are not ALL that defines me. Everything that has happened to me in life, everything that has happened to people in my life, and everything I have ever done affects how I live my life today. My actions are what define me, and I want to be defined as a caring, giving, strong-willed Christian woman who has overcome. Being an overcomer is a label I want to wear. Turning to God's word and my Christian roots reminds me who I am. Don't get me wrong, I was not miraculously healed from depression the first time I heard Lauren's song, but it started to help heal me one lyric at a time.

> You say I am loved when I can't feel a thing
> You say I am strong when I think I am weak
> And You say I am held when I am falling short
> And when I don't belong, oh, You say I am Yours
> And I believe
> What You say of me

The more I listen, memorize, and belt out the words in the car, the more I believe. I believe in the words, I believe in God's love, and I am starting to believe in myself. More importantly, I am starting to believe in God's word. I am loved, I am strong, and I belong here because I belong to *Him*, and *He* placed me on this Earth for His purpose. The apostle Paul reminds us through his second letter to the Corinthian church of "...our Lord Jesus Christ, the Father of compassion and the God of all comfort, who comforts us in all our troubles, so that we can comfort those in any trouble with the comfort we ourselves receive from God" (2 Corinthians 1:3-4). It is my hope that the comfort and strength I receive as *He* holds me tight through this mess can also comfort you.

The only thing that matters now is everything
You think of me
In You, I find my worth, in You, I find my identity
Taking all I have and now I'm laying it at Your feet
You have every failure, God, You'll have every
victory

My value comes from how *He* feels about me, not how *he* or *they* feel about me. So how do we know how *He* feels about us? We turn to *His* Word.

First off, we know we were made in God's image. To question how we look is to doubt *Him*. *He* made you the size, shape, color, and gender you are with a purpose. *He* chose your eye color, hair color, and skin color; *He* molded you inside and out to represent *Himself* in an Earthly form. Also let us not forget, *He* sent *His* Son to die for you and me. You know how someone who loves you might say, "I'd die for you"? Well, Jesus Christ actual did it. *He* died for you! That must make each of us pretty special. To validate you and myself even more, Proverbs 3:13–18 show us that if we honor the Lord with our wealth, understand *His* discipline, and study *His* word, we are priceless, rewarded, and a gift to anyone who lets us into their lives:

> Blessed our those who find wisdom, those who gain understanding, for she is more profitable than silver and yields better return than gold. She is more precious than rubies; nothing you desire can compare with her. Long life is in her right hand; in her left hand are riches and honor. Her ways are pleasant ways, and all her paths are peace. She is a tree of life to those who take hold of her; those who hold her fast will be blessed.

Though parts of King Solomon's instruction book, so to speak, are used as quotes and inspiration to build up women, I must be the bearer of bad news. The "she" in the above passage is actually used by the King of Israel as a pronoun referring to wisdom. However, what we can take away is not that we as women are all that, but that Miss Wisdom is, but that if we as Christian women gain that wisdom from trusting in the Lord, being faithful, submissive, and even fearful of *Him*, we will be or can become a "...wife of noble character...She is worth far more than rubies" (Proverbs 31:10). That time Solomon is speaking to real women, no personification of wisdom there. King Solomon goes on a bit later to remind us that "charm is deceptive, and beauty is fleeting; but a woman who fears the Lord is to be praised" (Psalm 31:30).

I believe what *He* says of me. I believe in *His* discipline, as I have witnessed it firsthand as I strayed too far. I believe that the more I study and write, the wiser I become, and this makes me a true gem. The wiser I become, the more I know I am enough, that I am *His*, that I am worthy, and that I am loved! I will lay every defeat and victory at His feet. Though I feel every circumstance in my entire life defines me, I will no longer let them form my identity. Say it with me loud enough for the neighbors to hear, "I am the daughter of the King. I am loved, I am *His*!"

Now think of your triggers. Are there songs you cannot listen to? Are there TV shows you cannot watch or places you do not want to go? How can God help you overcome these painful memories? Also, reflect on how you talk to yourself internally. Do you question your beauty or compare yourself to others? Do you sometimes or even oftentimes feel you are not enough? What or who makes you feel this way? Maybe it is time to give up some of those triggers, thoughts, or people. What will it take for you to believe you are beautifully and wonderfully made in God's image and that *He* has a plan for you? Before you journal about it, pray with me.

> Wise Heavenly Father, I fall at *Your* feet and give *You* my losses and my gains. I hear *You* say that I am *Yours*, and I believe it in my body and soul. Help me to continue to gain wisdom from *Your* word. "She" is a life partner I want to have with me always. Steer me to relationships with people who are wiser than I so that I may learn and guide me in teaching *Your* wisdom to others. When I am at my lowest, continue to fight off the voices in my head and open my eyes to all *You* see in me so that I may always believe. Humbly I pray. Amen

BE A JOURNALER!

BE A JOURNALER!

He Will Rescue You

"He heals the brokenhearted and binds up their wounds" (Psalm 147:3). Remember that Psalms is a book of songs. What a great resource for talking about how *hymns* help us learn about God, praise *Him*, and remind us how *He* loves us. Differing from Lauren's song "You Say," where she or we are singing out to God in our moments of sorrow and anguish, "I Will Rescue You" is written from God's point of view. *He* is singing to us!

> You are not hidden
> There's never been a moment you were forgotten
> You are not hopeless
> Though you have been broken, your innocence stolen

In line one *He* tells how *He* sought me out trying to hide on my closet floor. Line four is when *He* knew I was contemplating suicide. Lauren's knowledge of the Bible and God's love and promises are on full display in these lyrics. I close my eyes and see my God singing out to me that *He* understands my pain and that *He* sees me. The first verse shows where *He* found me and when *He* let me reflect a little on my pain. Previously I told you I would let you dwell in the misery a little bit because I think God let me. I believe it is part of the process of healing: to reflect, learn, and grow. Now this was only until I began to try to take the situation into my own hands. When I stopped believing *His* word and questioning my life and purpose, *He* stepped in.

I am not and was not innocent. I am and have always been a sinner, just as we all are. However, my innocence in love, marriage, and who I was and what I thought my life would become has been stolen. I truly believe in the sanctity of marriage. I truly believe in love. I truly believe in staying through the good times and the bad. But this decision has been taken away from me. I have lost my control over the situation and my beliefs in marriage. In this situation my innocence was my purity in marriage: never being divorced, never believing in divorce, never wanting a divorce. *He* reminds me in the last two verses that though my innocence was stolen, I am not broken, but I truly felt like I was shattered, not just my heart but my life as I knew it. What I have come to learn through studying my Bible and the lyrics of this song is that "The LORD is close to the brokenhearted and saves those who are crushed in spirit" (Psalm 34:18). Parts of me and my life are broken, injured, or wounded, but not ME. "He heals the brokenhearted and binds up their wounds"(Psalm 147:3), and I am slowly healing by *His* hands every day. Recovering from physical or mental agony is not a quick process and is usually a painful one. However, with the right support system and the Word of God, we can and will be cured. Even better, we can come out a stronger version of ourselves through our relationship with God.

> I hear you whisper underneath your breath
> I hear your S.O.S.
> I will send out an army to find you
> In the middle of the darkest night

It's true, I will rescue you

"Then call on me when you are in trouble, and I will rescue you, and you will give me glory"(Psalm 50:15 NLT). *He* hears our cries even when barely breathed; *He* hears our prayers even when we cannot seem to find the words. Reflect back to our conversation on the Holy Spirit and how *He* translates for us. The Holy Spirit is sending up our SOS to God. And as promised in the Psalms above as well as many other verses in book, *He* sent out an army to save me. I would be remiss to not mention the army that contains high-ranking officers known as my amazing mother, father, brother, and best friends as well as my aunts and cousins. However, it also contained a few new cadets that, although temporary, were an essential part of my rescue. Though the army God sent me is crucial to conquering the feelings of worthlessness and loneliness, *He* is the one who finds me every day, in every mood, and looks out for me. I should have known God would be there because *He* told us so in Ezekiel 34:11–12:

> I myself will search for my sheep and look after them. As a shepherd looks after his scattered flock when he is with them, so will I look after my sheep. I will rescue them from all the places where they were scattered on a day of clouds and darkness.

The metaphor above is used to compare Israel's leaders, who did not take care of *His* people and only cared for themselves, to shepherds and the flock as God's people. Today we can compare anything keeping us away from God, from doing *His* will, and following *His* words to the shepherds. *He* will come after you, just like *He* came for me!

There is no distance
That cannot be covered over and over
You're not defenseless
I'll be your shelter,
I'll be your armor
I will never stop marchin'
To reach you in the middle of the hardest fight
It's true,
I will rescue you

I am a child of God and with that comes the inability to ever win at hide-and-go-seek against *Him*. David tells us all about this in Psalm 139. We are shown through David's "song" that the Lord knows where we are physically, emotionally, and mentally. We were created body and soul by *Him*, and *He* knows our thoughts, movements, and desires even before we do. The distance mentioned in Lauren's words is metaphoric since *He* doesn't actually have to cover any ground to find us. *He* is always with us. However, when we slip into darkness such as depression or sin and assume God is not with us because light has no place there, *He* shines brightest. David shows there is nowhere we can escape *His* presence, not when we are high or when we are low, not when we are near or far, not when we are under water or above it. Christians are assured by the apostle Paul that no matter what we struggle with internally, we are not alone when stating, "For I am convinced that neither death nor life, neither angels nor demons, neither the present nor the future, nor any powers, neither height nor depth, nor anything else in all creation, will be able to separate us from the love God that is in Christ Jesus our Lord" (Romans 8:38-39). That love is what finds us no matter our distance, and it protects us, just like armor protects a soldier going into battle. Having the knowledge that love of the Father and Son shelters and protects me aids me in surviving this fight.

This fight is, at least at the moment, the hardest fight of my life. *He* is marchin', every day God is marching toward me and for me. On the days I cannot get out of bed, answer the phone, or see a better tomorrow, *He* marches on. With each and every step, God is rescuing me from the pain and sorrow. With every step *He* gets closer to me and helps me see that better tomorrow. With every step *He* gives me hope.

Your questions to ponder here are about your relationship with *Him*. Do you believe God when *He* says *He* hears your suffering and that *He* will always come find you in your darkness? Is there a time you can recall when *He* did? Or maybe you are thinking of a time that you feel *He* didn't? If so, is it that *He* did not rescue you, or is it that *He* did not do it the way you thought *He* should? Do you have faith in *His* plan?

> Mighty Conqueror, thank *You* for always knowing where I am and meeting me there. Thank *You* for not letting darkness within me and around me keep you away. I am grateful for *Your* undying love and willingness to forgive and protect me in any and every situation. Thank *You* for sending *Your* Son to save me and for forgiving me. Thank *You* for giving me the Holy Spirit to intercede for me when I am weak and do not know what to say to You. I ask *You* to continue marching on my behalf when I am weary and keep me wrapped in *Your* armor of protection and love. In *Your* divine name I pray. Amen.

BE A JOURNALER!

_____
_____
_____
_____
_____
_____
_____
_____
_____
_____
_____
_____
_____
_____
_____
_____
_____
_____
_____
_____
_____
_____
_____
_____
_____

BE A JOURNALER!

_____

_____

_____

_____

_____

_____

_____

_____

_____

_____

_____

_____

_____

_____

_____

_____

_____

_____

_____

_____

_____

_____

_____

_____

_____

_____

PART 3-3:

Trust in Him

I remember as a child having to put a cassette tape into a cassette player and fast forward, play, fast forward, play, "ah man!", rewind, play until I found the song I wanted to hear. As a teenage girl, it was usually a silly love song about a boy who I had googly eyes for or one that I thought had broken my heart forever. I also remember using those same cassettes and the same player to record songs of my brother. These songs portrayed his feeling about any number of political or cultural issues. Just kidding, they too were usually about "love" and some girl. Love songs have been around as long as music. They have been made popular by romantic movies, wedding dances, and social media. Every genre of music has love songs, including Christian music. Love songs are not always about happy, perfect love. Sometimes they are about heartbreak or a harmonious plea for someone to come back. I am unsure if Lauren Daigle's "Trust In You" was meant as a love song, but to me it is. What better way to show God our love than by truly trusting in *Him*.

> Letting go of every single dream
> I lay each one down at Your feet
> Every moment of my wandering

Never changes what You see
I've tried to win this war, I confess
My hands are weary, I need Your rest
Mighty warrior, king of the fight
No matter what I face, You're by my side
When You don't move the mountains I'm need-
ing You to move
When You don't part the waters I wish I could
walk through
When You don't give the answers as I cry out to You
I will trust in You
Truth is, You know what tomorrow brings
There's not a day ahead You have not seen
So in all things be my life and breath
I want what You want, Lord, and nothing less
You are my strength and comfort
You are my steady hand
You are my firm foundation
 The rock on which I stand
Your ways are always higher
Your plans are always good
There's not a place where I'll go
You've not already stood

Can you imagine if someone said those words to you? What a statement of love! The words show true submission. I sing out these lyrics louder than any others because this is where I falter daily. I know God knows all. I know *He* has seen my future. I know *He* has plans for me. However, that stinkin' devil gets in my head, and the controlling part of me takes over. I struggle to let go and let God because I feel the need to know and handle everything right now and by myself. I am not 100% where this obsessive need for control part of me came from, but with the help of therapy, I believe it started in my childhood when my brother had a bad accident and snowballed throughout life as every little thing I could not control came my way. It is a difficult thing to understand if one does not suffer from the same urges. Though I feel a need to be in control of almost everything, I long for someone to take that power from me and lead me because the burden is so heavy. Needing to take charge and wanting to are two very different things. I thought my spouse would be that man, and to some extent, sometimes *he* was until *he* wasn't anymore. The Christian woman who had been hiding deep inside me was longing for a spouse who would lead me not only financially but emotionally and spiritually.

A true apology comes from omittance of your wrong. Some of the lyrics above represent how I (and maybe you) tried to fight the battle on my own and failed. This is an apology to God for even thinking I held that kind of power. Furthermore, I feel apologetic for asking *Him* to move mountains and part waters I wanted *Him* to, not asking *Him* to do for me what He wanted to and knew was best. First, I wanted my husband back, then I wanted *him* to feel pain like I did; I regretfully prayed for vengeance. When I realized what I was praying for was wrong and started praying for God to do *His* will in my life, I felt my prayers being answered, I felt my heart beginning to heal, and I felt my life getting better. This is when I began to trust in *Him*.

TRUST. That is a little word with a big meaning, and it takes a great deal of faith to put your full trust into someone, even if that someone is God. I have already shared with you multiple stories from the Bible that show where people put their trust in God, even when the situation seemed crazy or impossible, like David and Goliath and Job and his suffering, and were rewarded in *His* time for their faith. However, there are so many more inspiring examples of God's mercy, God's greatness, and God's follow-through with his promises when you keep the faith. Genesis shows us Abraham's and Sarah's faith when they longed for a child, and this same prayer is answered through Zechariah's and Elizabeth's faith as seen in the book of Luke. I bet you may be somewhat familiar with Daniel and the lion's den when his faith protected *him* from being torn apart by the lions. You may also have heard of Shadrach, Meshach, and Abednego, another story of God's protection from the book of Daniel. The three men were sent into the fire by the Babylonian king because they refused to worship a golden idol. Three were sent in, but four bodies walked through the fire, the fourth being God's son sent to bring them out of the blazing furnace unharmed. Not only did their faith protect them, but it also influenced others as even the king himself saw the son of God and *His* protection of *His* people and recognized *Him* as the one true God. Stories like these are hard to relate to today as we do not often get thrown into a literal lion's den or furnace. However, they are metaphors for what does and can happen to us, from the accidents or natural disasters to the tragedies or depressions; God will walk through it all with us if we just have faith in *Him*.

The last story I want to bring to your attention is a simple one that we as ladies can relate to even today, the woman who bled for twelve years. The four Gospels, Matthew, Mark, Luke, and John all write astonishing accounts of Jesus's superhuman healing power during his time walking here on Earth. Mark tells the quick story of the bleeding woman the Lord healed right after *He* had healed the demon-possessed man and right before *He* raised the dead little girl. As the crowd of people grew around Jesus, the suffering woman, who had been to many doctors and was only getting worse, reached out across the masses to try to at least graze *Him*, believing, "... 'If I just touch his clothes, I will be healed.' Immediately her bleeding stopped, and she felt in her body that she was freed from her suffering" (Mark 5:28-29). Jesus felt a jolt as the power left *His* body and went into someone else. There were so many people around *Him*, he had to ask who touched *Him*. The woman fell at Jesus's feet fearfully admitting what she had done. Though fear was not necessary as "he said to her, 'Daughter, your faith has healed you. Go in peace and be freed from suffering'" (Mark 5:34). What a wonderful God we serve! *He* rewards us for our faith. *He* is our strength, comfort, our steady hand, our foundation, and our rock on which we stand.

I know, I know the hardest part of this is the unanswered prayers thing. Having true faith in God means understanding that *He* knows what is best for us and sometimes that means our prayers are not answered. Remember, though, *He* sees what we do not, *He* hears what we cannot, and *He* knows our past and our future. When I think of true love and faith, I often think of having children or even fur babies. They truly love and have faith that we will do what is best for them. They depend on and need us, and since we know more than them, it may not always be to give them what they want, but we try to make sure they have what they need. Disclaimer, this changes as your children become teenagers. They no longer think we know everything; as a matter of fact, they think we know nothing, so the love is still there but their faith not so much.

When you are ready to put your true faith into God, and hopefully you are now or at least you are feeling closer to being ready, sing out this love song to *Him* or use the lines below to write your own lyrics. Tell *Him* you are sorry for trying to do life your way and give *Him* the power to work in your life as he sees fit. Then do your best to live a life where you mean these words every day and do not worry if you fail, because you will, it is guaranteed. I fail. However, I fail less and less every day as I pray for God's forgiveness and guidance. How awesome is it that we have a forgiving Father?

> Lord of Love, please forgive me for sinning against *You*. Forgive me for the days when my faith is lacking and help me to remember that I am *Your* daughter, the daughter of the one true King. Help my trust in *You* to grow every day and guide me in showing *You* through my patience and understanding of *Your* plan. Lastly, please show me how to always wear my faith as a badge of honor so that I may be a witness to others of your abiding love for us, forgiveness of us, and faithfulness to us. In *Your* Loving name I pray. Amen.

BE A JOURNALER!

BE A JOURNALER!

_____
_____
_____
_____
_____
_____
_____
_____
_____
_____
_____
_____
_____
_____
_____
_____
_____
_____
_____
_____
_____
_____
_____
_____

It's Only the Beginning

don't know your story. I do not know if *he* left you or you left *him* or if you are still all in, fighting for your love. I am not sure if you are dating, engaged, or married still. I am unaware if there was abuse, neglect, infidelity, or abandonment. I definitely am not sure if reconciliation is a possibility for you. Maybe you are reading this just to learn to heal from something totally different. However, here is what I do know; you will be all right. I know that you can be forgiven for any and all of your sins and that God already has a bright future in store for you. I know that with a strong foundation built with the Father, the Son, and the Holy Spirit, you can and will have stronger, healthier relationships in the future. In the beginning of trauma, we don't want to hear things will be OK. We want to and deserve to mourn and wallow in our self-pity. Allow it to happen, but then pull yourself out of it and move forward. What other choice do you have? Feel like you can't do it alone? Neither could I. I had to reach out to friends, family, and a therapist to get myself straightened out and moving on again. There will be times when you stumble. The filing of the paperwork, the selling of the house, the holidays (geez, do those stink), the random symbols or memories of what used to be that pop up in the cabinet or on your social media feed are going to be rough. Then there is the dread associated with what is to come: the finalization of the divorce, when *he* starts dating again, and again I say those holidays (this one is gonna sting for a few years I predict). It is valid to feel sad but just don't lose yourself in the sadness for too long. Be vulnerable and ask for support. Open up your Bible for guidance and pray for courage. It sounds cliché, but it really does work, I promise! I never imagined eight, six, or even four months ago I would be where I am today. I am strong. But I am not strong on my own. I almost feel awkward when people commend me for being strong, though, because it isn't me, it is *Him*.

Remember to love above all else. Love yourself and love others, all others. Even those who have wronged you, actually, especially those who have wronged you. Love is so much more than a word or feeling, it is a way of life. "...let us not love with words or speech but with actions and in truth" (1 John 3:18). I used to feel guilty for still loving my ex-husband. I felt that saying I would always love *him* would make me, in a weird sort of way, unfaithful to my future boyfriend or husband. But remember there are different types of love. *he* will just go into a new category in my heart and brain now. Think of it as a file folder titled Love. Inside that folder are other folders with headings such as The Trinity, Strangers, Frenemies, Colleagues, Church Family, Friends, Family, Romantic Partners, and Self. Even those folders can drop down with more detailed folders. For example, the love I have for my great-aunt is different from that of the love of my mother. Make sense?

Now I want you to put an imaginary asterisk next to the Love folder in your mind that reads Self. Sometimes, especially for women, this is the hardest one to access. Physically, emotionally, and every other -ly, we struggle to love things about ourselves. Well stop it right now, young lady! You are beautiful in the eyes of the Lord! I am not just saying that, it is biblical. You were made in the essence of God *Himself*. You were sculpted by *His* prefect hands. Do not get tied up in outward appearance, as I know it is easy to do in the world we live in today. "Your beauty should not come from outward adornment, such as elaborate hairstyles and the wearing of gold jewelry or fine clothes. Rather it should be that of your inner self, the unfading beauty of a gentle and quiet spirit, which is of great worth in God's sight" (1 Peter 3:3-4). Beauty comes from the inside. I know you have heard that your whole life. But what does it mean? A woman who has confidence, poise, and happiness when she walks and talks is beautiful. Confidence is one of the most attractive things about a woman. Put yourself in the company of women like that, confident Christian women (not to be confused with egotistical or vain). You know what *they* say about the company you keep. When you are struggling, depressed, angry, or any other of the ugly emotions, love yourself through it. Allow it for a short time. Set a "Get Over It" alarm on your phone. When it buzzes, jump up with a plan to do something for yourself. Have fun! You deserve this. Get a new hobby. Play a sport, scrapbook, learn an instrument, write, or try it all. Just make sure to make time for you. Remember that change takes time, healing is messy, but you are strong. I never knew how strong I was until I had no other choice. You have no other choice, friend, be strong!

Being strong for my children was difficult, at times they were the ones being strong for me. But now, to repay them, I am going to be nice to their father (insert cringe). It is my Godly duty as a mother to model for them what forgiveness and love looks like, even in the toughest of situations. My ex and I used to say, jokingly of course, when other people got divorced that we wouldn't be like that. We would want to be friends and get along. Easier said than done when it actually happens, though. I will get there, some semblance of there anyway. I mean, I get better every time we talk. This is only through the grace of God. I feel *Him* inside me taking away the pain, anger, and sadness. It is crazy and can only be understood by you once it happens. It is peace. Peace is difficult to explain. It is a feeling of calm, almost a numbness, but in a good way. Oh wait, I know how to explain it. Peace is like a shot of Novocain to your heart or a big dose of ibuprofen. The pain is taken away! People would call me after I met with *him* with sadness and concern in their voices and say, "Honey, are you OK? I bet that was hard." Almost as if they expected me to break down and cry to them, which I did at first, a lot! But not very often now. It is God! *He* reminds me in my studies about watching my tongue, speaking with love and not anger, forgiveness, and raising Godly children. We are reminded by Paul that children are to "'honor thy mother and father'— which is the first commandment with a promise— 'so that it may go well with you and that you may enjoy long life on earth'" (Ephesians 6:2–3). If I bash the man who broke my heart to my children, this will most definitely affect their relationship with *him*, as if this whole thing hasn't caused enough damage already. This is not what I want for my children. I do not want *them* to go against God's word to honor *him*, forgive *him*, and love *him*. Because my amazingly, awesome kids have stepped up for me, I will step up for them. Plus, this is the law of Christ, "LOVE," no ifs, ands, or buts. My new triangle has been made whole with my boys filling in that once-missing angle for now. Someday they will create their own triangle with a woman God has chosen for *them*. How they treat her will reflect how

God works in their lives and how I have raised *them*. I will not let this divorce ruin their outlook on love and marriage!

Divorce should not ruin your outlook either! Maybe you have hope for your marriage or current relationship. Maybe it won't end badly. Maybe it does, and afterward you get back together. Hey, it happens. In one of the books I have read, it actually did happen to the author. Those books gave me hope for a long time. I mean hope is good, right? But now I try not to think that way because it hurt, and I know it is the not the case for me now, and I am actually better because of it. However, sometimes falling apart is what brings people closer together and more importantly closer to God. *He* restores, *He* repairs, and *He* renews. *He* did these many times in the Bible. Oftentimes to entire nations or groups of people. Now I just put things in God's hands and try not to wish for a future I know nothing about but that I stay faithful and on the path that God has laid for me. "Trust in the LORD with all your heart and lean not on your own understanding; in all your ways submit to him, and he will make your paths straight" (Proverbs 3:5–6).

Lastly, I beg you, please do not give up on human contact and a loving relationship on this side of heaven just because you have been hurt. "...Don't let your hearts be troubled and do not be afraid" (John 14:27). I am not cynical to love. Some people are after a devastating divorce or loss of any kind but not me. I love love! I know God has a man for me. I will continue to be still and wait for *Him* to reveal *him* to me. I can only pray it will be a love like no other. The one we read about in the Bible. The one like my grandparents had and that my parents share. We are given advice by King Solomon of Israel in Proverbs to "...guard your heart, for everything you do flows from it" (4:23). This does not mean do not let anyone in! It means to be cautious of how you use it and who you let into it.

King Solomon is revered as one of the wisest men in ancient times. Maybe *his* advice is worthy of taking, then. When you wish to be saved, healed from all your past discretions, and are ready to live a Christian life, you say the sinner's prayer. You are inviting Jesus Christ into your heart. A happy heart is a healthy heart and a better place for *Him* to reside, don't you think? Now is time to say so long to the old you, the old life, and the old man but hello to all the extraordinary possibilities. Goodbyes are hard, but sometimes they are necessary in order to say hello to something or even someone new. It is never too late to live happily ever after. I believe in you. I know you have this, and *He* has you! I love you all!

If you so feel convicted to do so or are just curious what it would sound like, here is an example of a prayer to say if you are not already a Christian and would like to be saved. Remember, though, you can put your own twist on it, your own "lyrics." *He* is anxious to connect with you personally. It doesn't have to be fancy. Just simple and to the point. Let Him know your heart.

Lord Jesus, I know you are the Son of God. I am a sinner. Please forgive me and renew my soul and heal my heart so that it is worthy for you to live in forever. Thank *You* for dying on the cross to wash away my sins. I believe *You* rose from the dead, and I want to trust in *You*, walk in faith, and have eternal life. In *Your* name I pray. Amen.

> If you declare with your mouth, 'Jesus is Lord,' and believe in your heart that God raised him from the dead, you will be saved. For it is with your heart that you believe and are justified, and it is with your mouth that you profess your faith and are saved. (Romans 10:9–10)

Acknowledgments

When I think of all the support I have had over the last year while trudging through the D word and writing this book, I am overwhelmed with joy. I am so blessed to have so many supportive people in my life. I have mentioned my boys a great deal already but would be remiss to not say it again; they are my everything! They, like me, were raised in church, but as my ex and I began to fade away from church, we didn't think of what we were doing to them. However, they persevered, and through this their closeness to God has only grown. I know they too will get lost sometimes, but I am confident in God's word and the groundwork that has already been laid for them to find their way back to *Him*. My boys encourage me every day and never lose faith in *His* plan. They are definitely God's children, and I am so anxious to see what *He* has in store from them. I am complimented regularly on the character of my boys and give credit for this where it is due. First to the Heavenly Father and *His* word and second to my amazing role-model parents.

My mom is a beacon of *His* light. She has the strongest faith of any woman I know, and she has had many situations in her life to cause her doubt. But she stands firm. She cries with me, laughs with me, and talks with me daily. She is more than my mom; she is my best friend for life! Her dedication to my father and example of a Godly wife is inspiring. She has always honored *him*, shown *him* love, respect, and care. She never gave up on *him*. My daddy is not too bad *himself*. *he* has grown into a wonderful man of God right before my eyes, and I have never been prouder of *him* than for that. Through this ordeal, when I was left feeling rejected by the man that I thought God had given me to be my forever protector, I realized I was mistaken. My daddy is the man on Earth that God gave me for that! *his* love is unconditional. *his* arms make me feel safe. The way *he* treats my mother comes straight out of the Bible. *he* adores her, respects her, and has patience and forgiveness for her, no matter the circumstance. OK, well the patience thing may be an ongoing work in progress, but at least *he* tries. My poor ex, what a difficult task it must have been for *him* to try to measure up to my daddy. To Mom and Dad, I simply say thank you for EVERYHTING!

Family is where my heart is strong. My aunts and cousins have supported me from afar. They call, send me encouraging texts and verses from the Bible. Some were used in this book. My aunt and cousin have at times in my life felt more like a second mom and sister. They just get me and know what I need often before I do. I think my aunts prayed harder for me than I did for myself. I am in love with all their relationships with the Lord and how their faith stays strong. My family's love for me is undeniable. It has molded me into the Christian woman I am today. I love you all and will never be able to explain how much you mean to me.

Next, I would like to show appreciation to my small group. A group of amazing women from different walks of life, different age groups, and different stages of their lives who all have managed to affect mine. They showed up every week to learn about God, *His* son, and the Bible. They shared their infinite wisdom, their joys and sorrows, and their prayers. It is amazing how God works. I promise you I would be writing the part of the book about friendship and next thing you know our group was studying friendship. Often, I would question something I had written in my head, and then I would spiral down an emotional writer's block staircase. A week later one of them would say something that would answer my question, even without knowing, and give me the ability to move forward with my writing. "For where two or three gather in my name, there am I with them" (Matthew 18:20). I feel his presence every time we meet. This group brought me out of my comfort zone and helped me to be vulnerable; I am so humbled my them. WCC ladies, I cannot thank you enough for your friendships and support during the most difficult time in my life.

Oddly enough I would also like to thank my ex-husband. Did you notice in the last section I stopped referring to *him* as my soon-to-be ex? This book has taken me years to complete, as it has taken me years to heal. Not only is that acceptable and normal, but it has also led me to be able to honestly write this paragraph. My ex gave me twenty-plus amazing years and two fantastic kids, well, now they are young adults. *he* is partially responsible after all for my boys' good genes and some of their amazing characteristics. Sometimes the most difficult part is that I see *him* in them, the good and unfortunately some of the bad (ugh!). I wish we had done some things differently, and I definitely wish our marriage would have turned out differently. The fact that we were so awesome together for so many years is what has made this almost unbearable and completely unbelievable. I was *his* biggest fan. *he* was my best friend; I know this is true because it said it on our wedding napkins. Hard to believe but I do not regret one second of it. Where does regret get us anyway? I hate that we lost our way and made some bad decisions. I know I am the better for it. I truly pray someday *he* will be as well.

Second to last, I would like to show my appreciation for my brother. *he* gives some advice, but more importantly *he* just listens and always provides a strong shoulder to cry on. We share history, a story like no other (hopefully a collaborative book in the future). We both have had reasons to doubt and lose faith, but even in our darkest days, God brings us back to *Him*. Together my brother and I are stronger. *he* is a very intellectual guy and has so much love to share with the world. *his* God-given gift of music has not even begun to reach the millions I feel it should. Thanks, Bubba, for always having my back!

Saving the best for last, I want to thank God for giving me *His* love by offering up *His* son. Thank *You* for leaving the ninety-nine for me! In case you are not familiar with this story, Jesus tells a parable in Matthew 18:12–14:

> What do you think? If a man owns a hundred sheep, and one of them wanders away, will he not leave the ninety-nine on the hills and go to look for the one who wandered off? And if he finds it, truly I tell you, he is happier about that one sheep than about the ninety-nine that did not wander off. In the same way your Father in heaven is not willing that any of these little ones should perish.

God does regular head counts of *His* children and knows when one is missing. Just as an Earthly father or mother would do when on vacation with the family or when getting everyone to a basement during a tornado. Think if one of your children or beloved pets runs away or gets lost. Wouldn't you go find them? So, thank *You*, Heavenly Father, for finding me when I wandered off and for bringing me back to *You*.

Words cannot even express my gratitude to Jesus Christ for dying on the cross for my sins and showing me what it looks like to give and receive unconditional love. Thank *You* for modeling friendship, forgiveness, humility, vulnerability, and sacrifice. I am grateful to have hope and faith in my life thanks to *You*. I pray that if it is the will of *You* and the Father, this book is successful in reaching others who have wandered off, feel afraid, have questions, or have uncertainty in their lives. It is my hope that it will give them some peace and reassurance in *Your* plan. Thank *You*, Lord, thank *You*, thank *You*, thank *You* for being my *Him*.

About the Author

Kristina is an author, speaker, educator, and mentor living just north of Atlanta, Georgia. Most of her free time over the last twenty years has been watching her two, now grown, sons play baseball, football, and golf. Now that Kristina has more time for herself, God has called her to share *His* word and her journey of how *He* has worked in her life. She feels by being single, married, divorced, single again but in her 40s, and now engaged at almost 50, she can relate to many women at different stages of their lives. *him, Him, and hymn* is her first book of hopefully many to come to help women feel understood, supported, and loved by her and God. Please find out more about Kristina, her family, upcoming books, and events by connecting with her at:

Website: www.kristinakay.net
Facebook: Kristina Kay-Finding Life His Way
Instagram: @KristinaKay03

Be on the lookout for the next book in her Trilogy Series: *Ladies, the Lord, and Love Songs.*